MINDFUL MEANDERING
Stress Relieving Adult Coloring Book
by Serena King

This Mindful Meandering coloring book is designed to ignite your creativity, while providing a platform for a relaxing, deeply meditative experience. As you add vivid color to the various illustrations, we invite you to notice the elegant beauty in the patterns of nature. Ultimately, it is our sincere hope that this coloring book will inspire, calm, and center you. Namaste.

To keep up-to-date with the new adult coloring books as they become available, we invite you to check out serenaking.com coloring books.

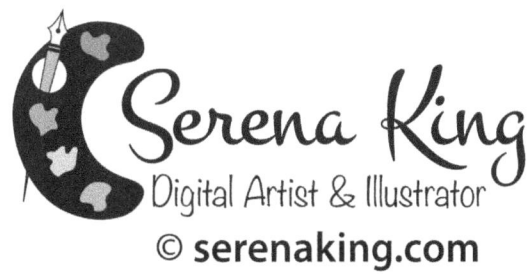

Serena King
Digital Artist & Illustrator
© serenaking.com

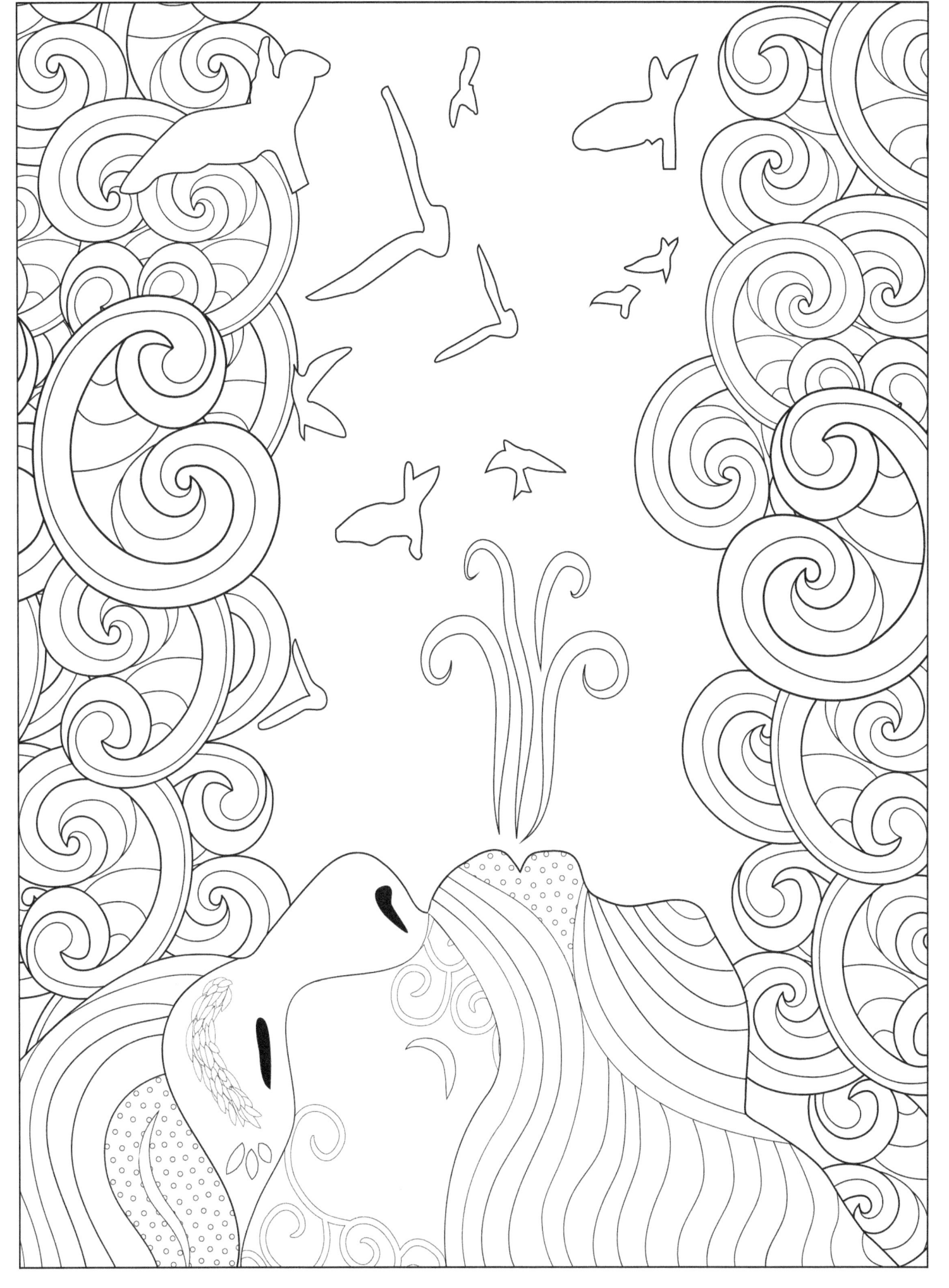

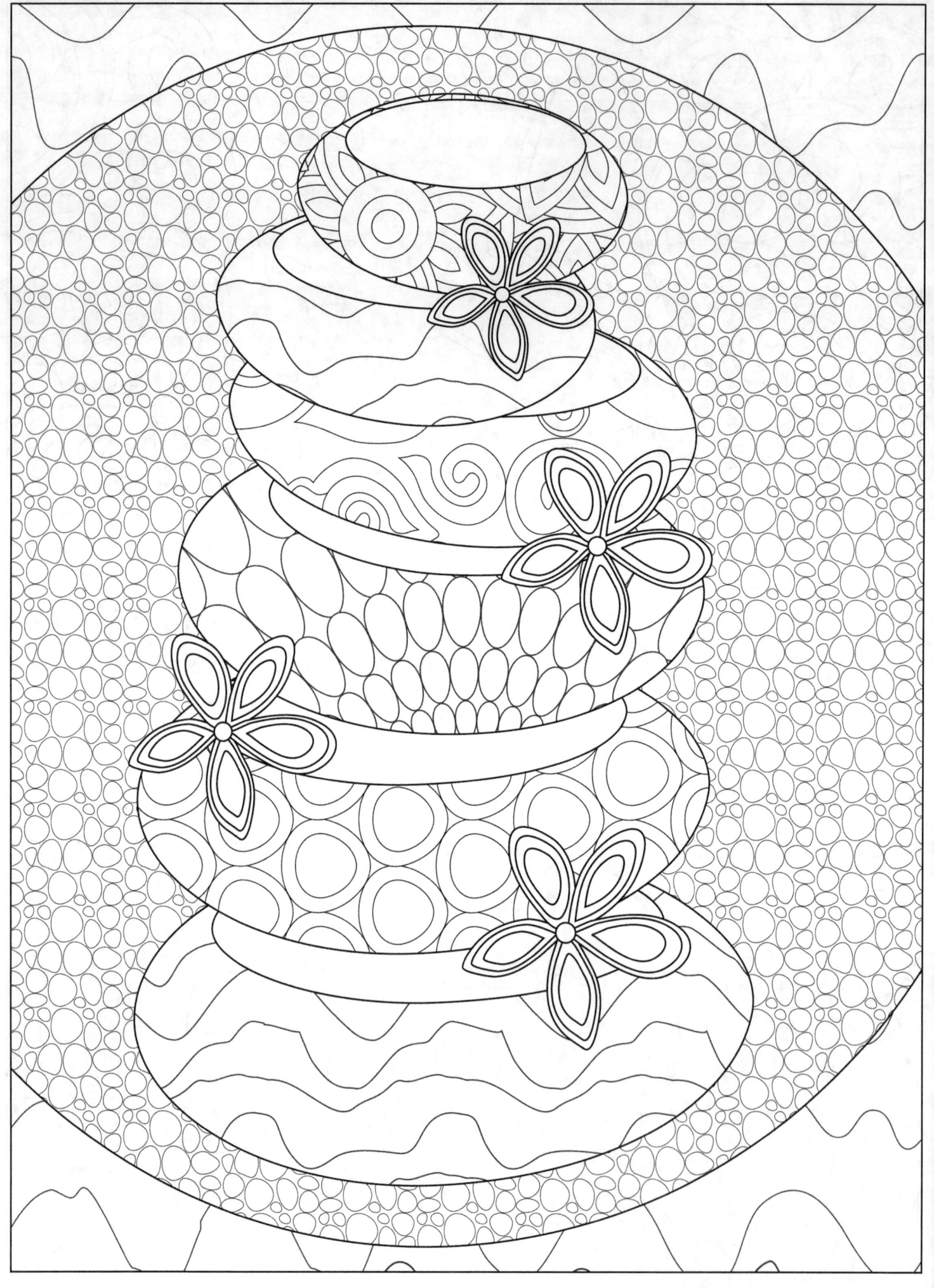

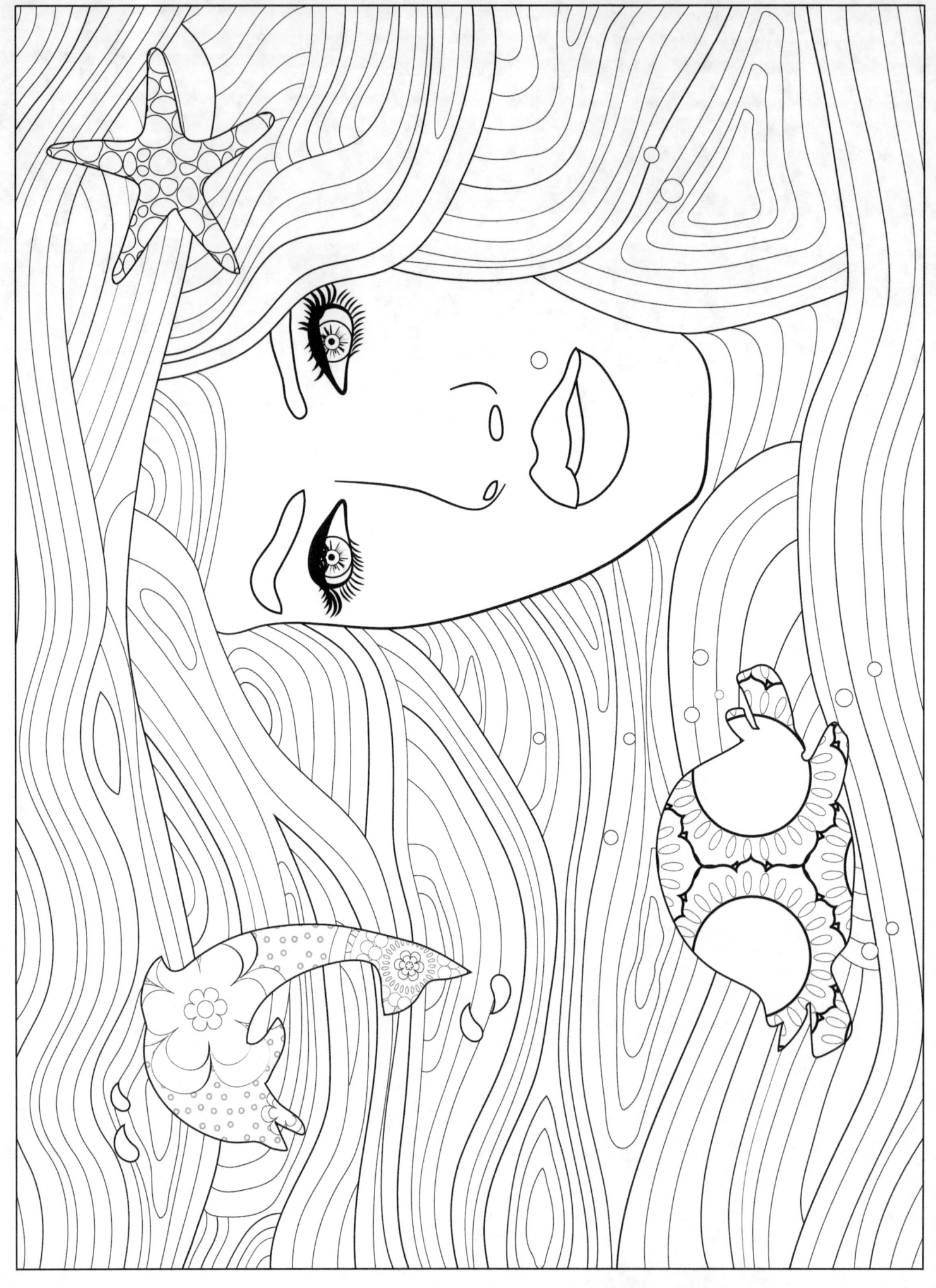

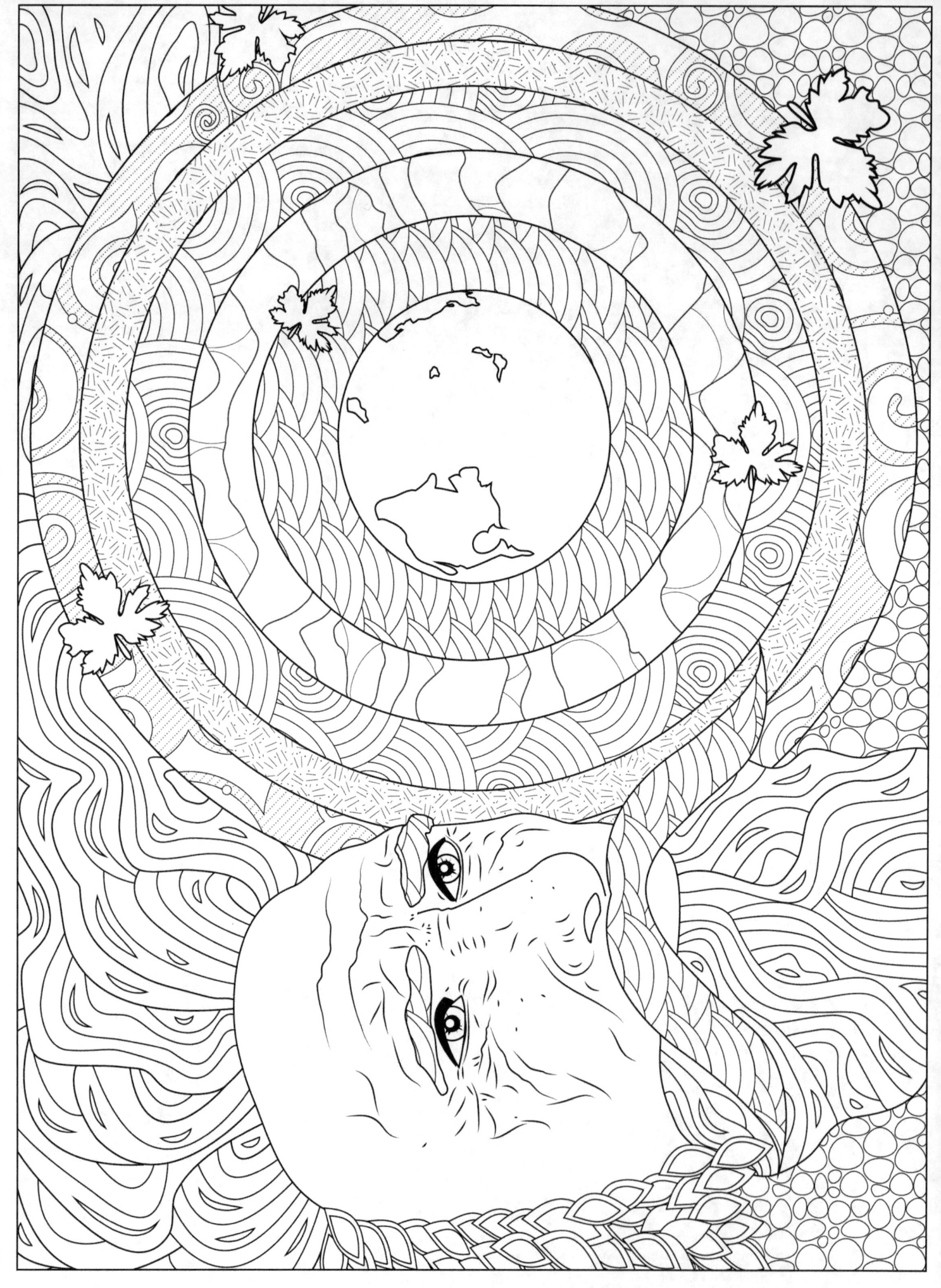

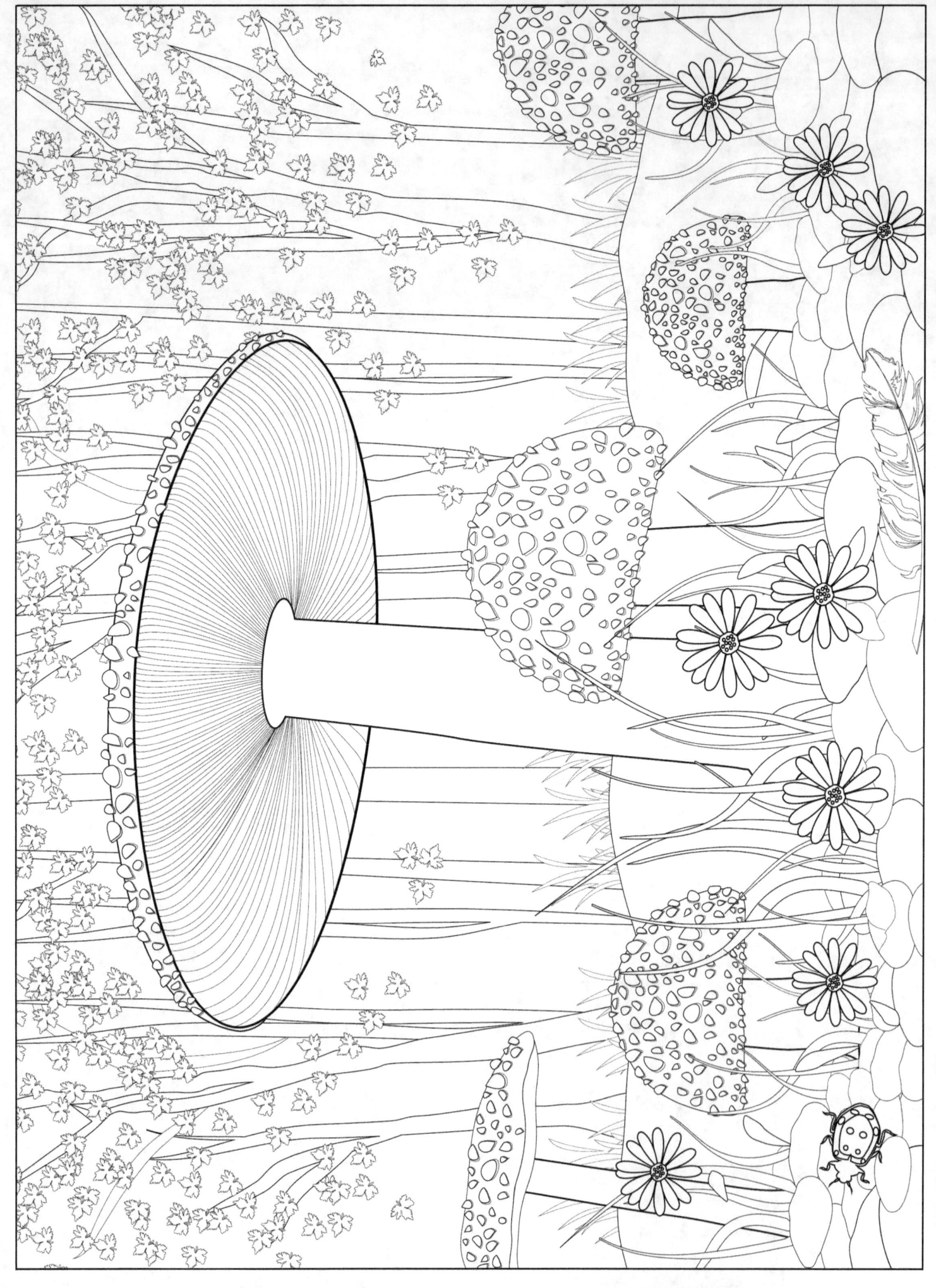

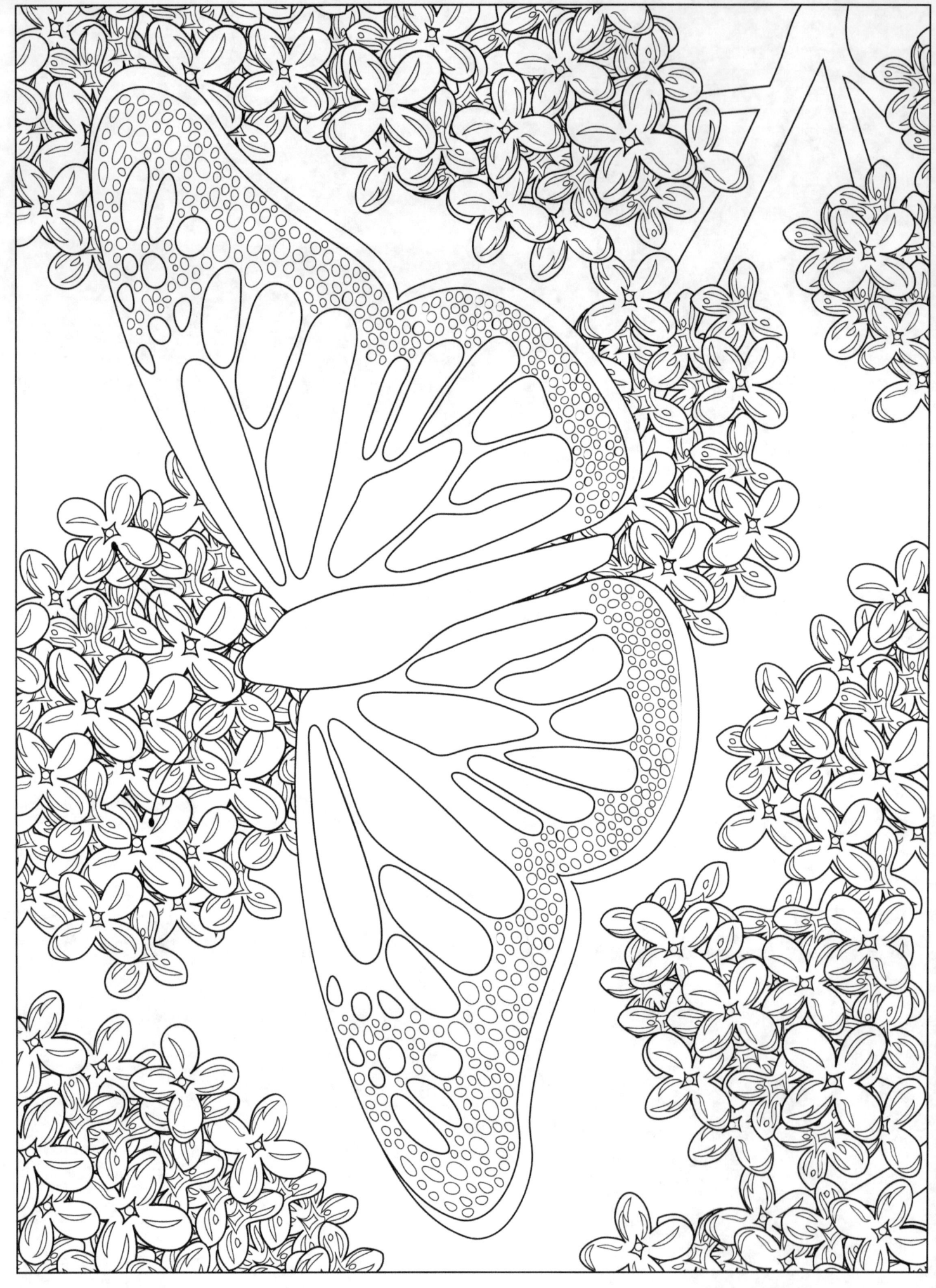

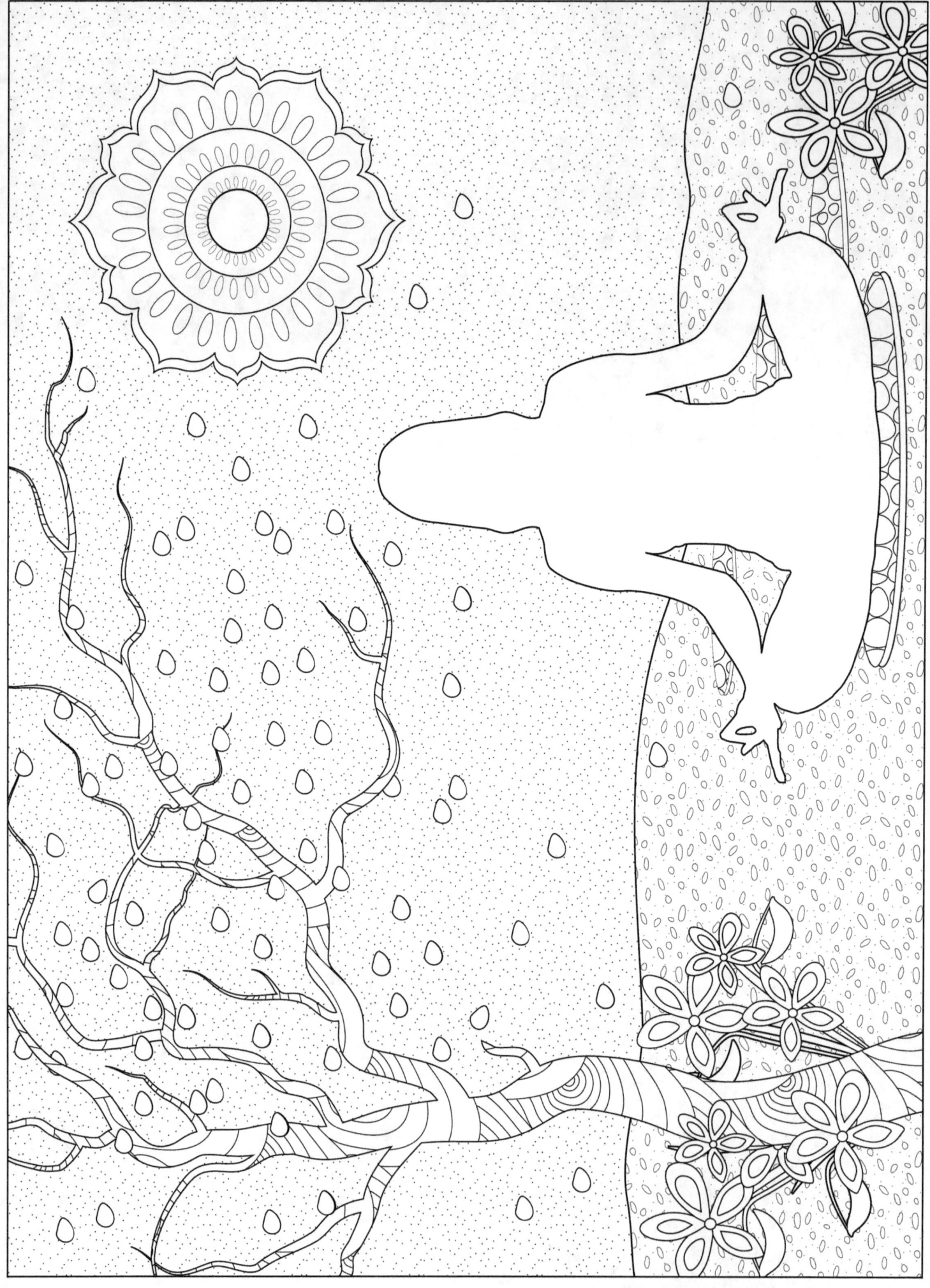

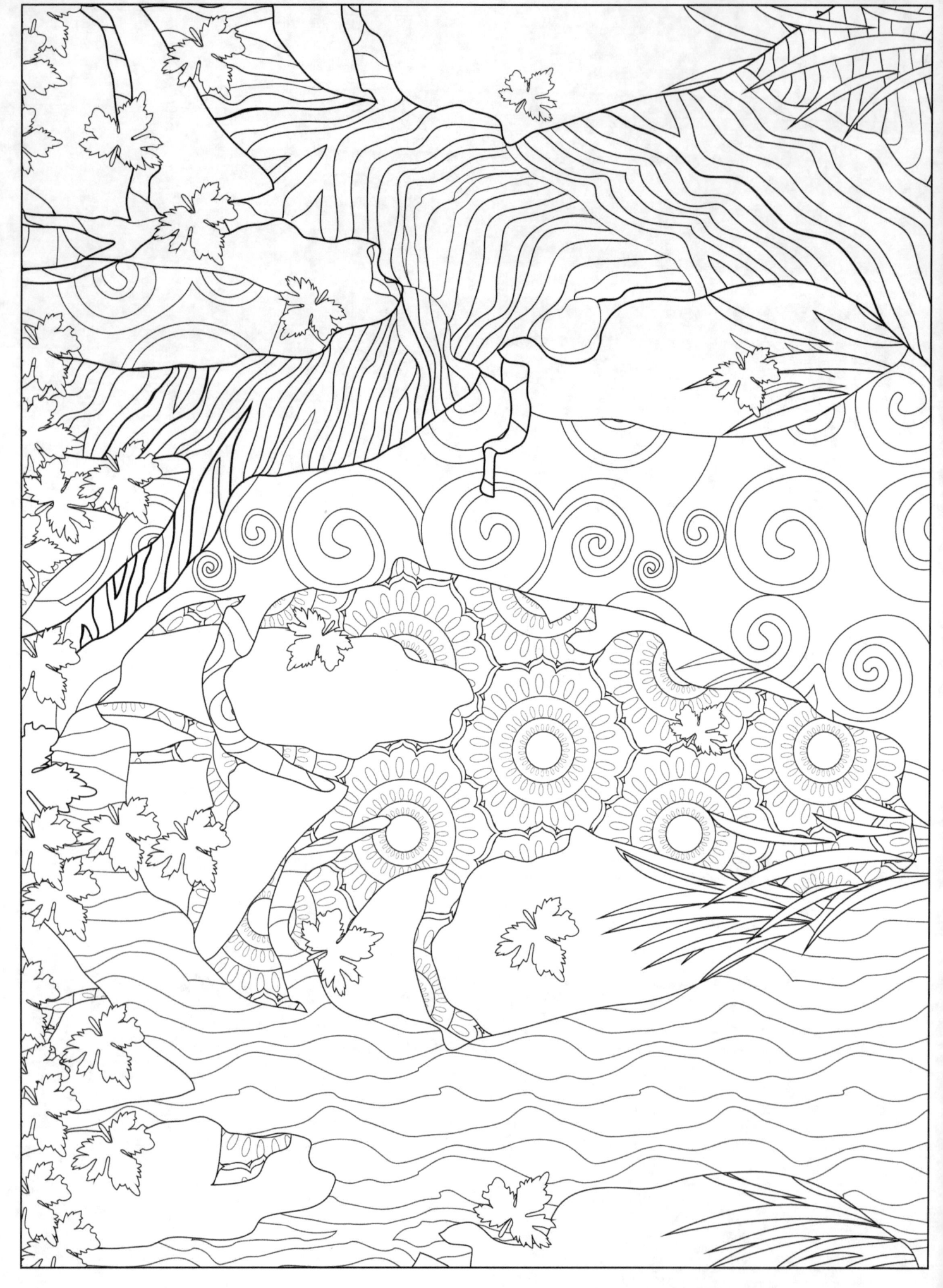

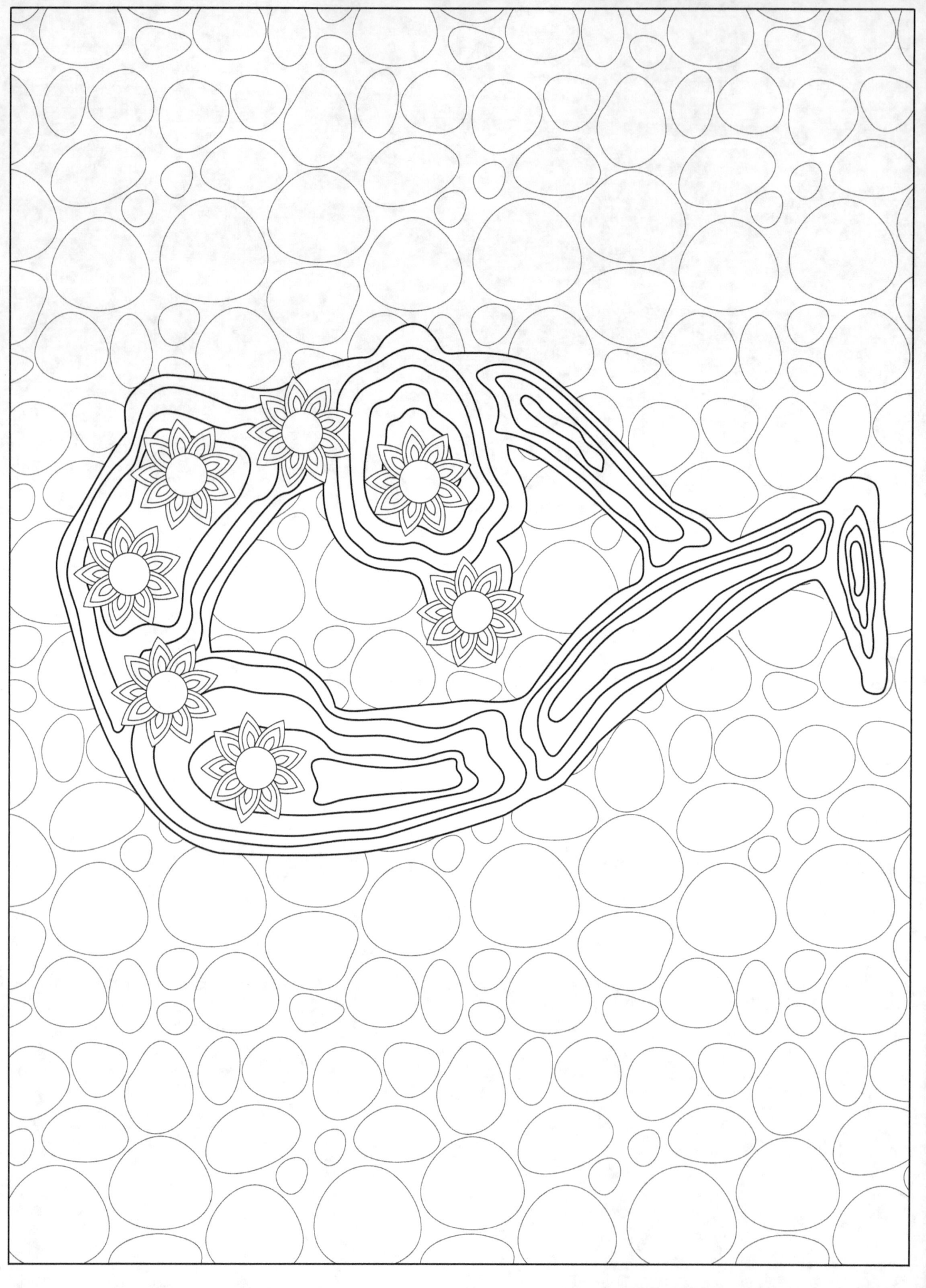

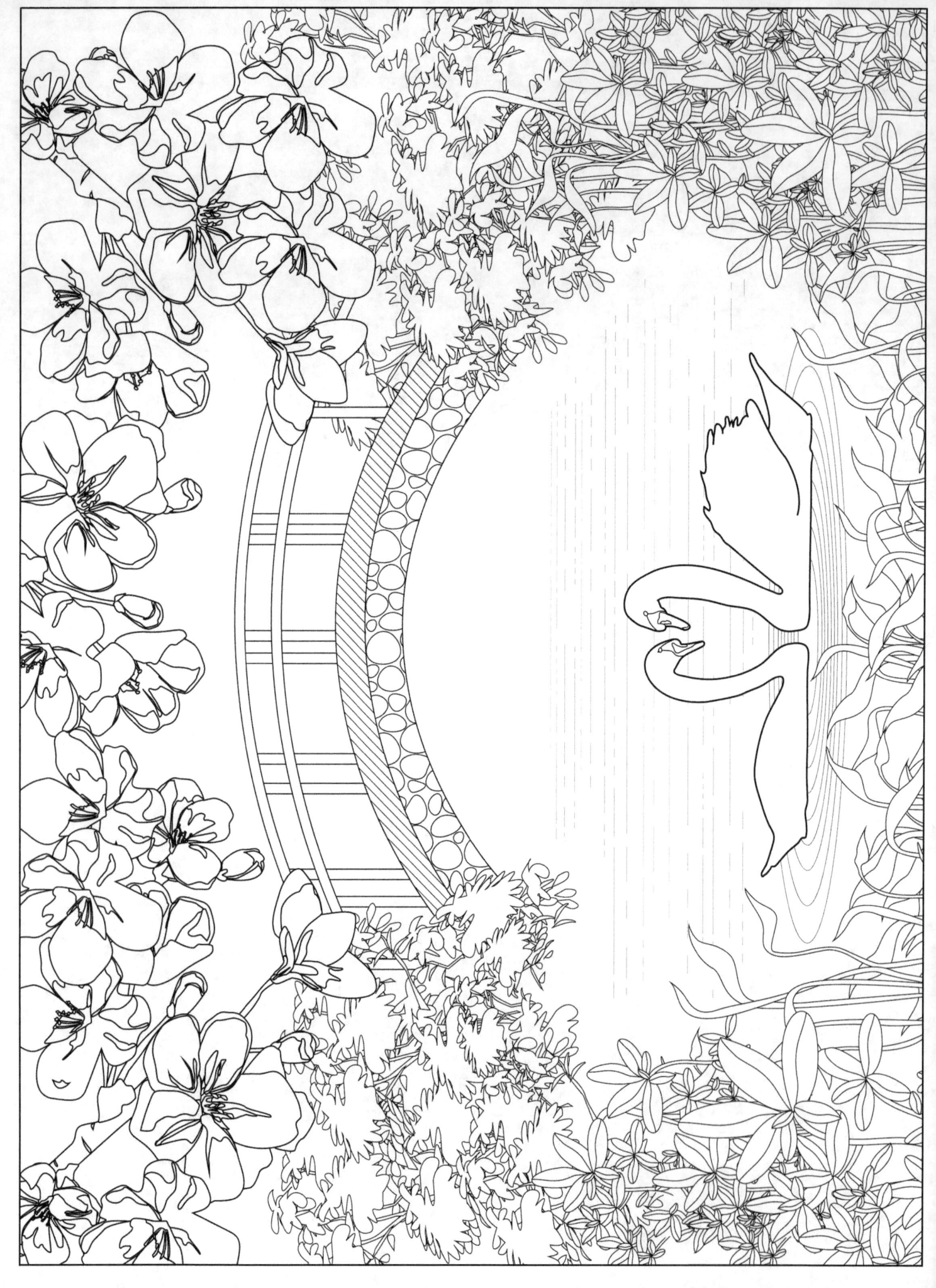

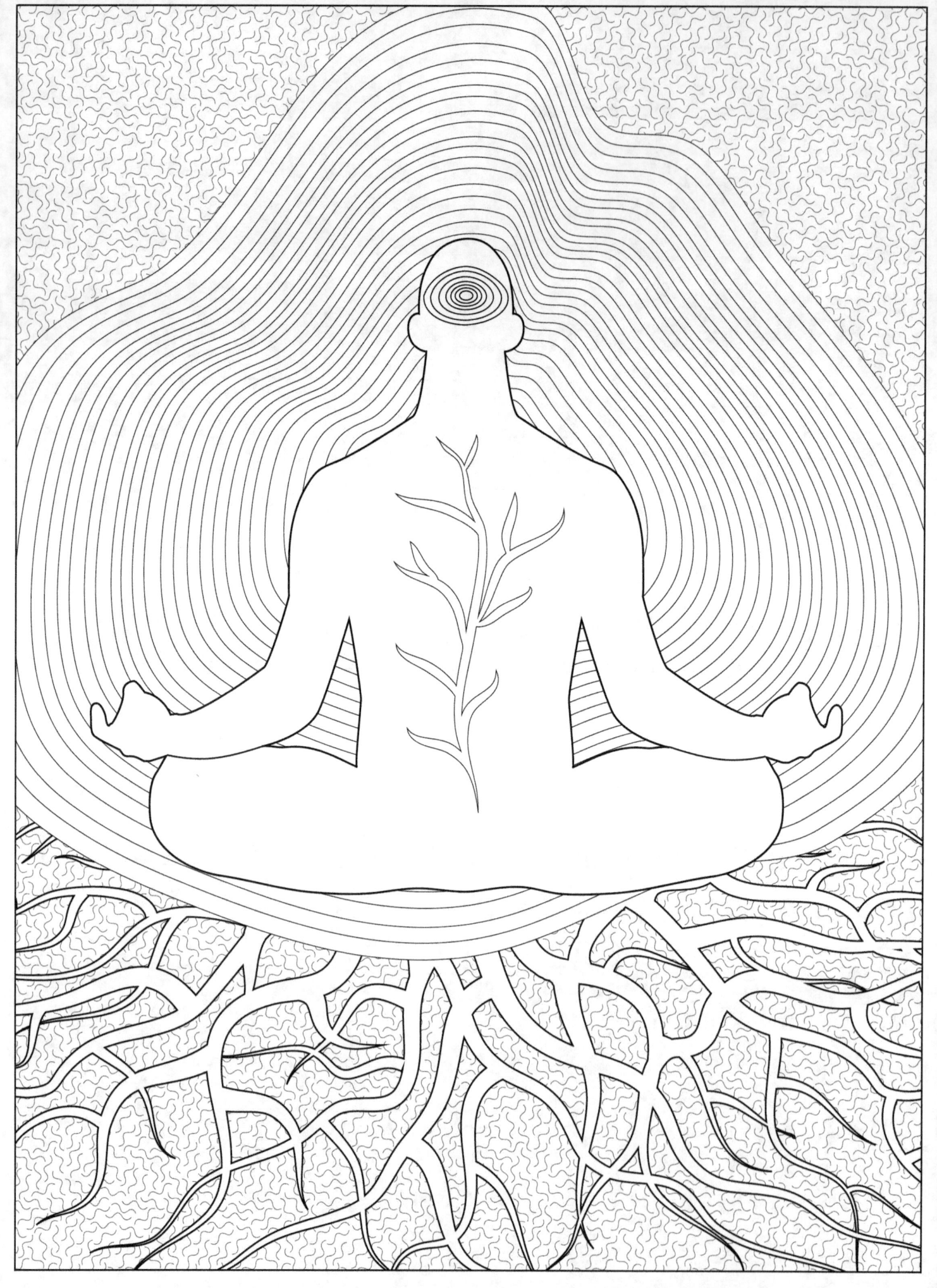

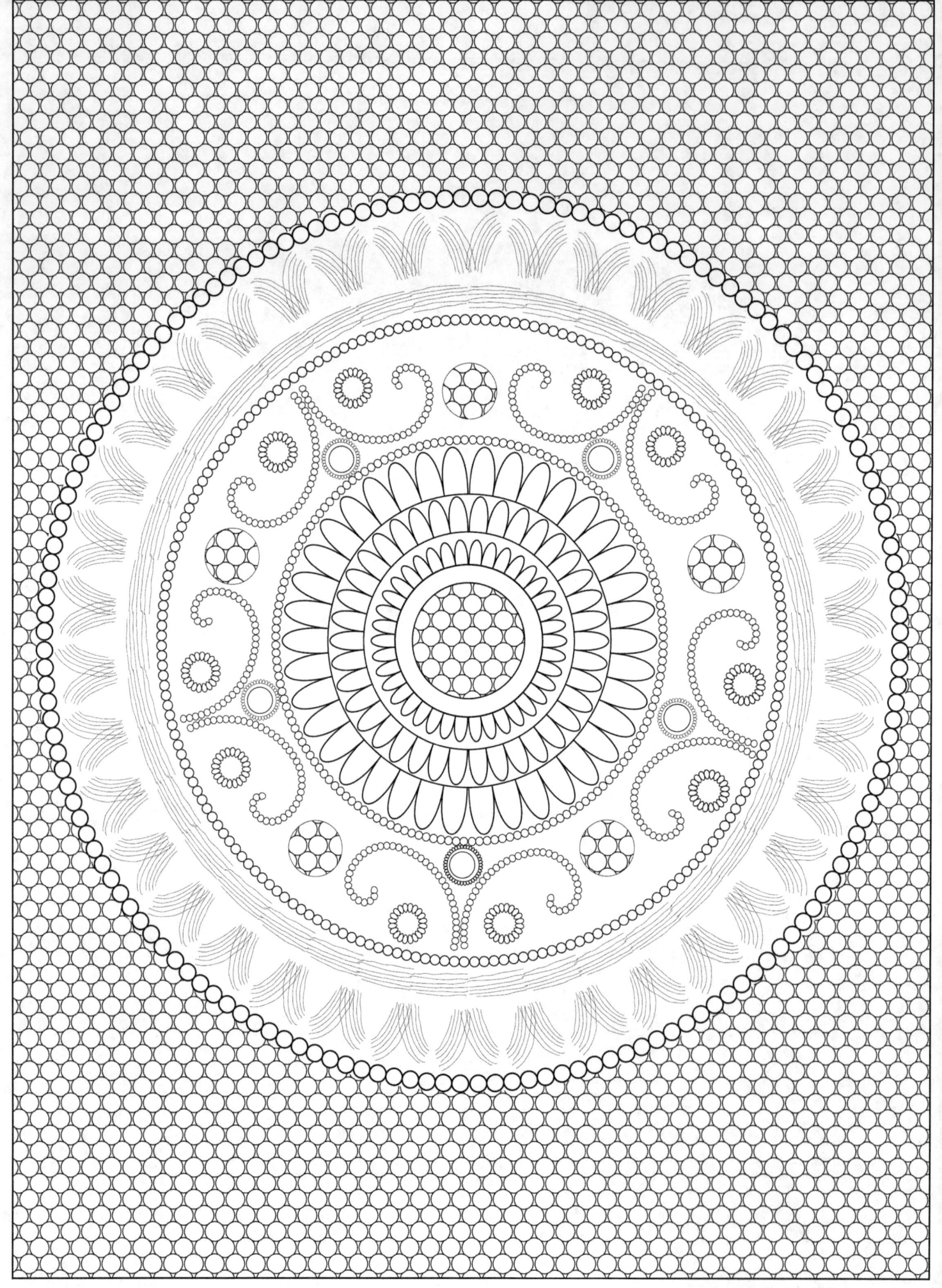

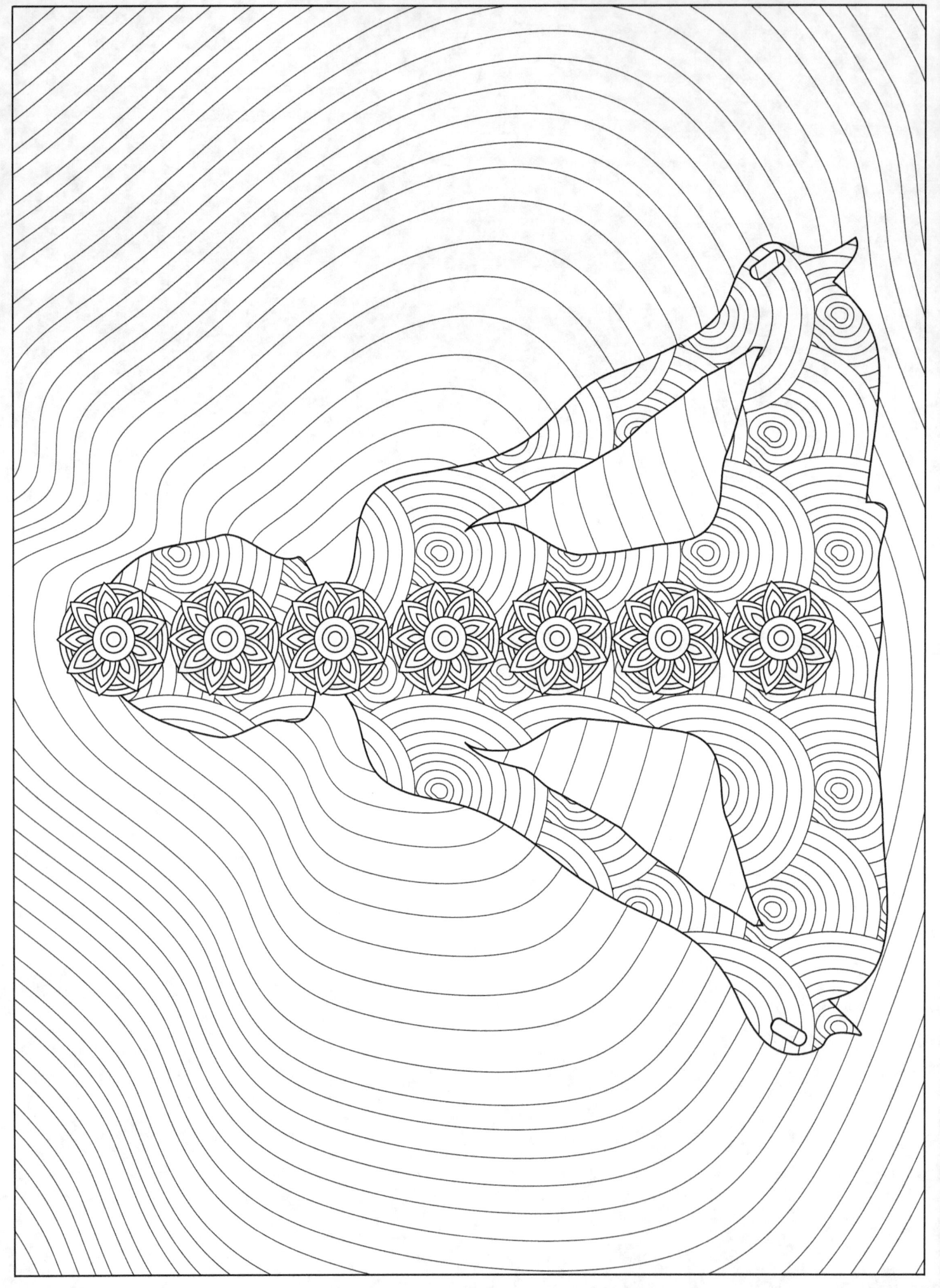

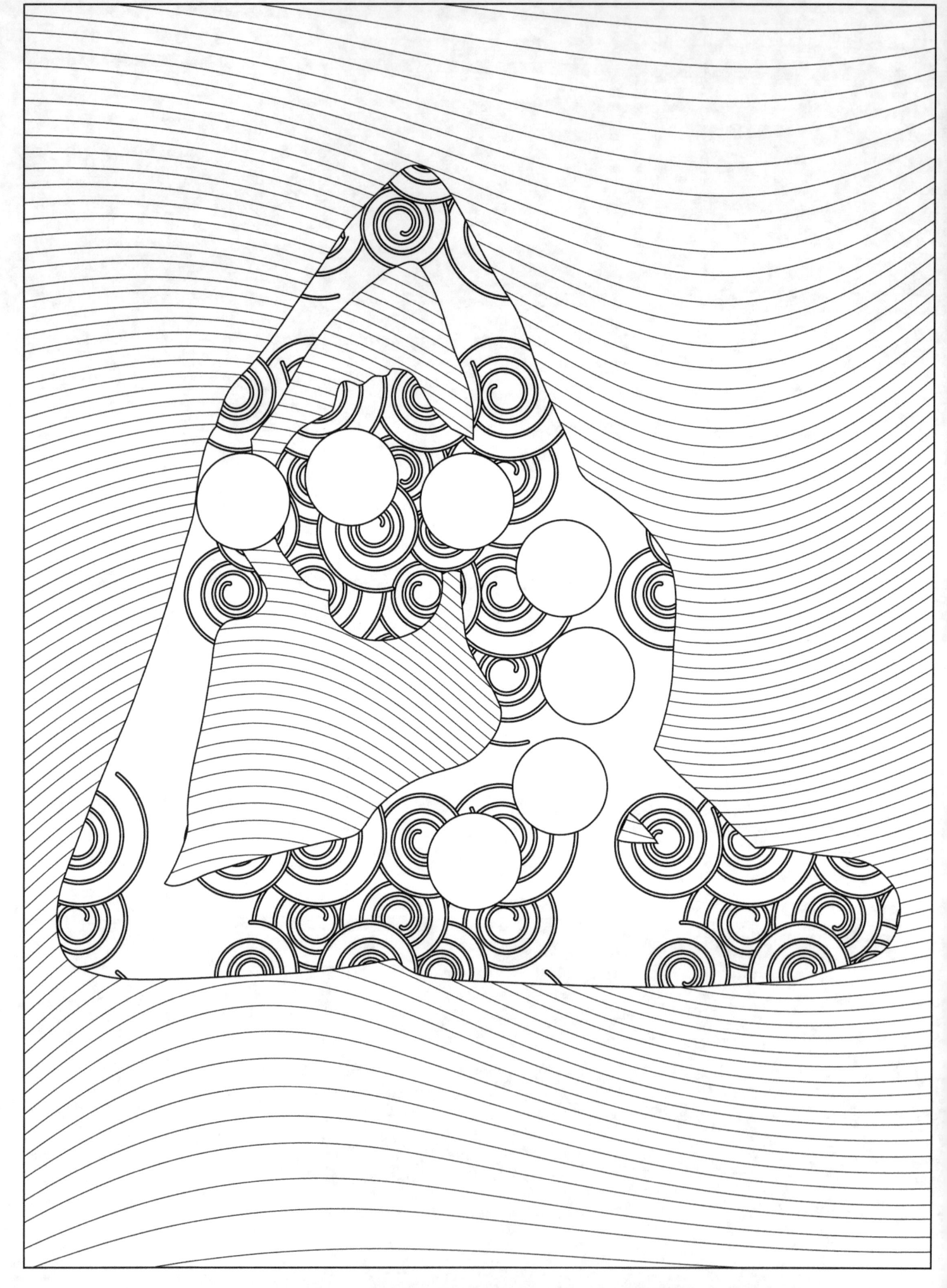

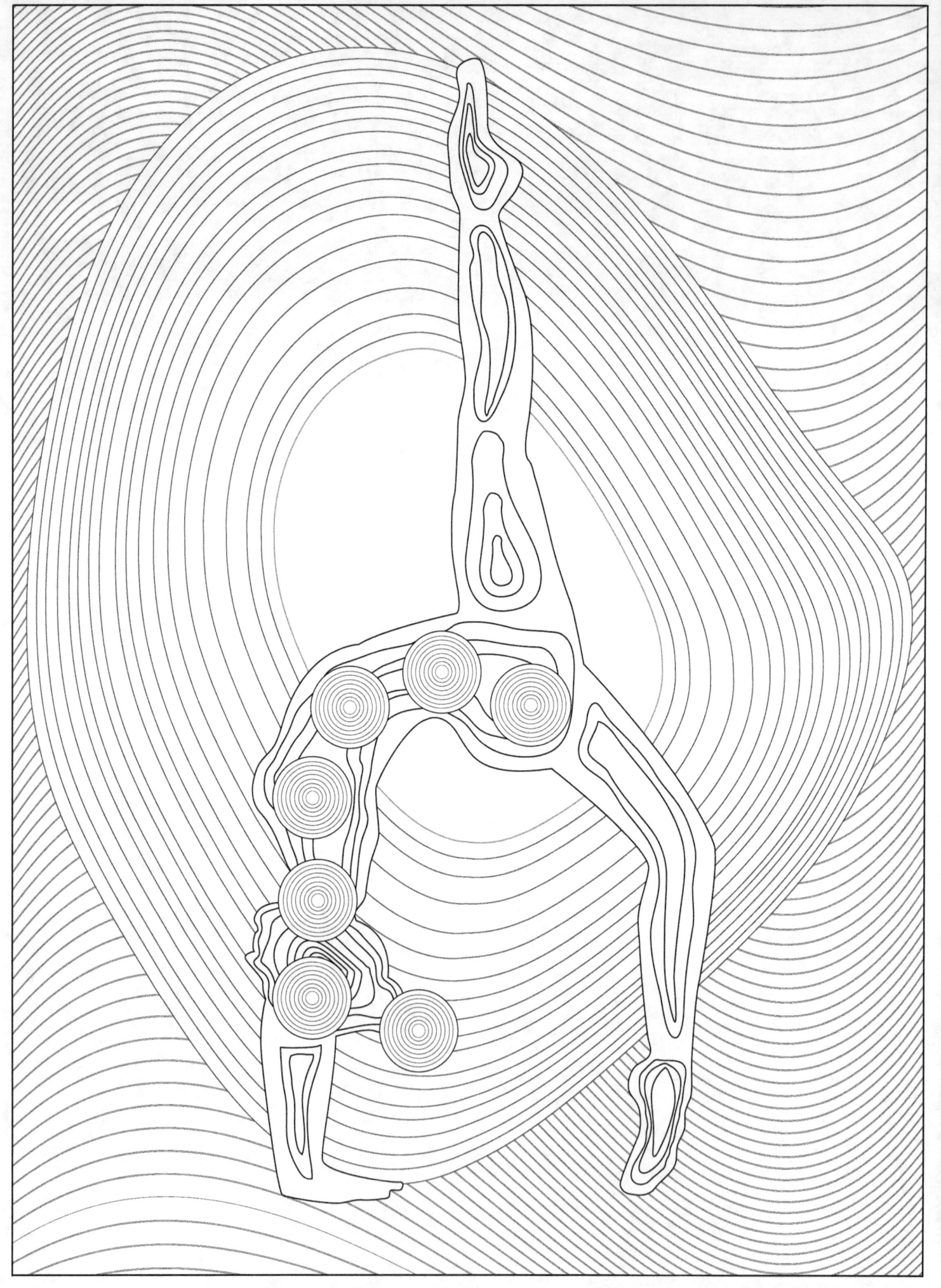

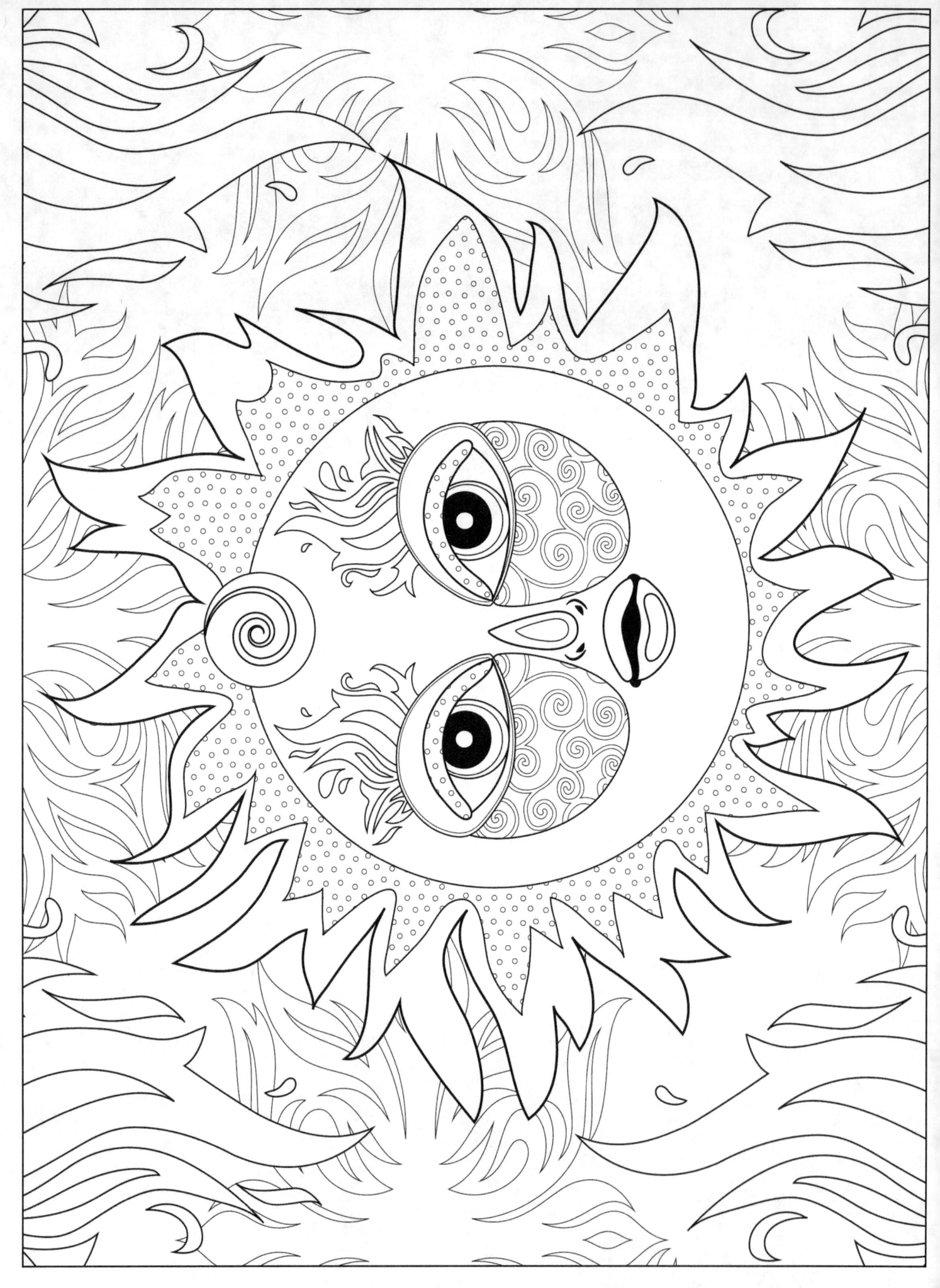

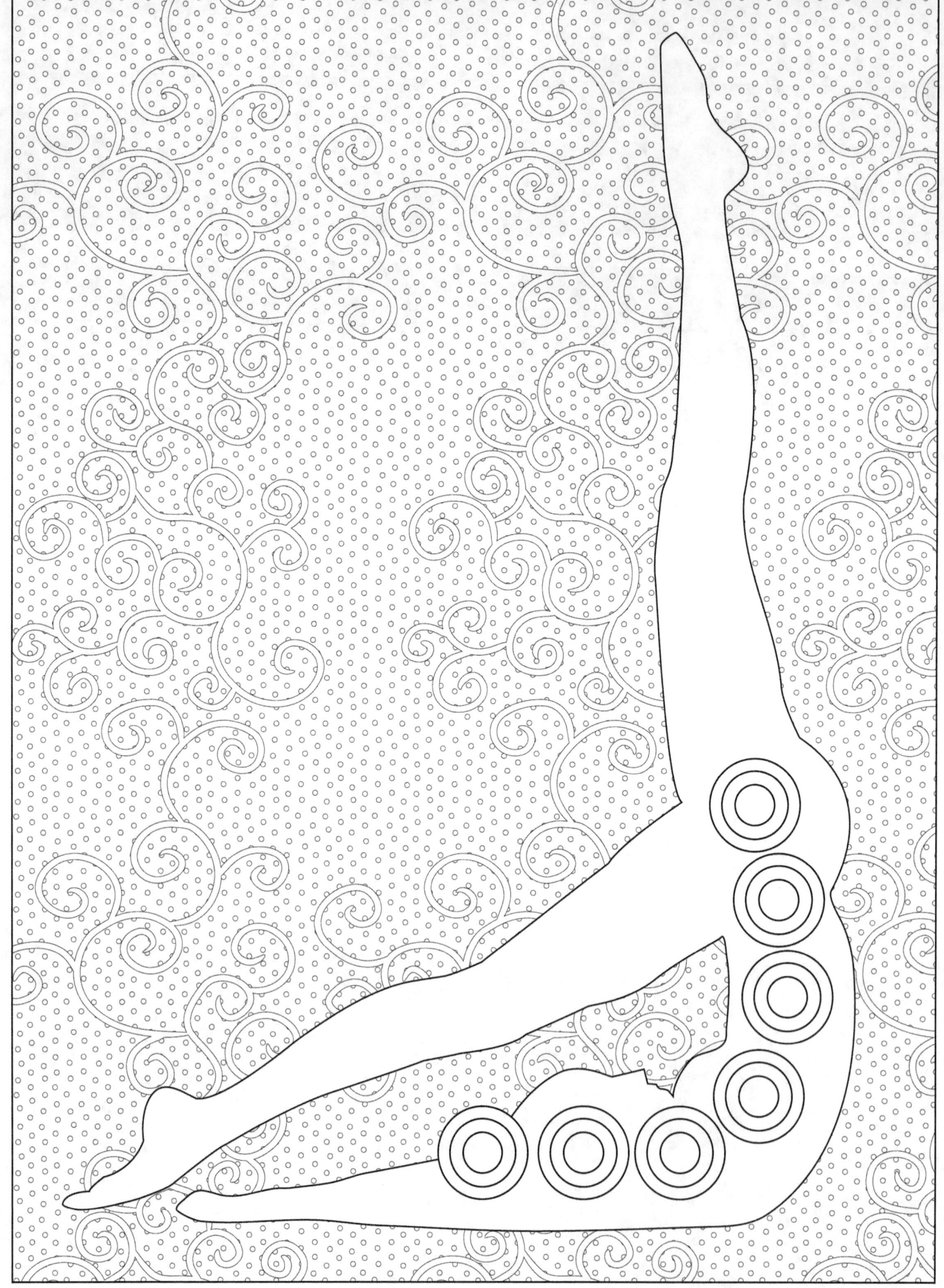

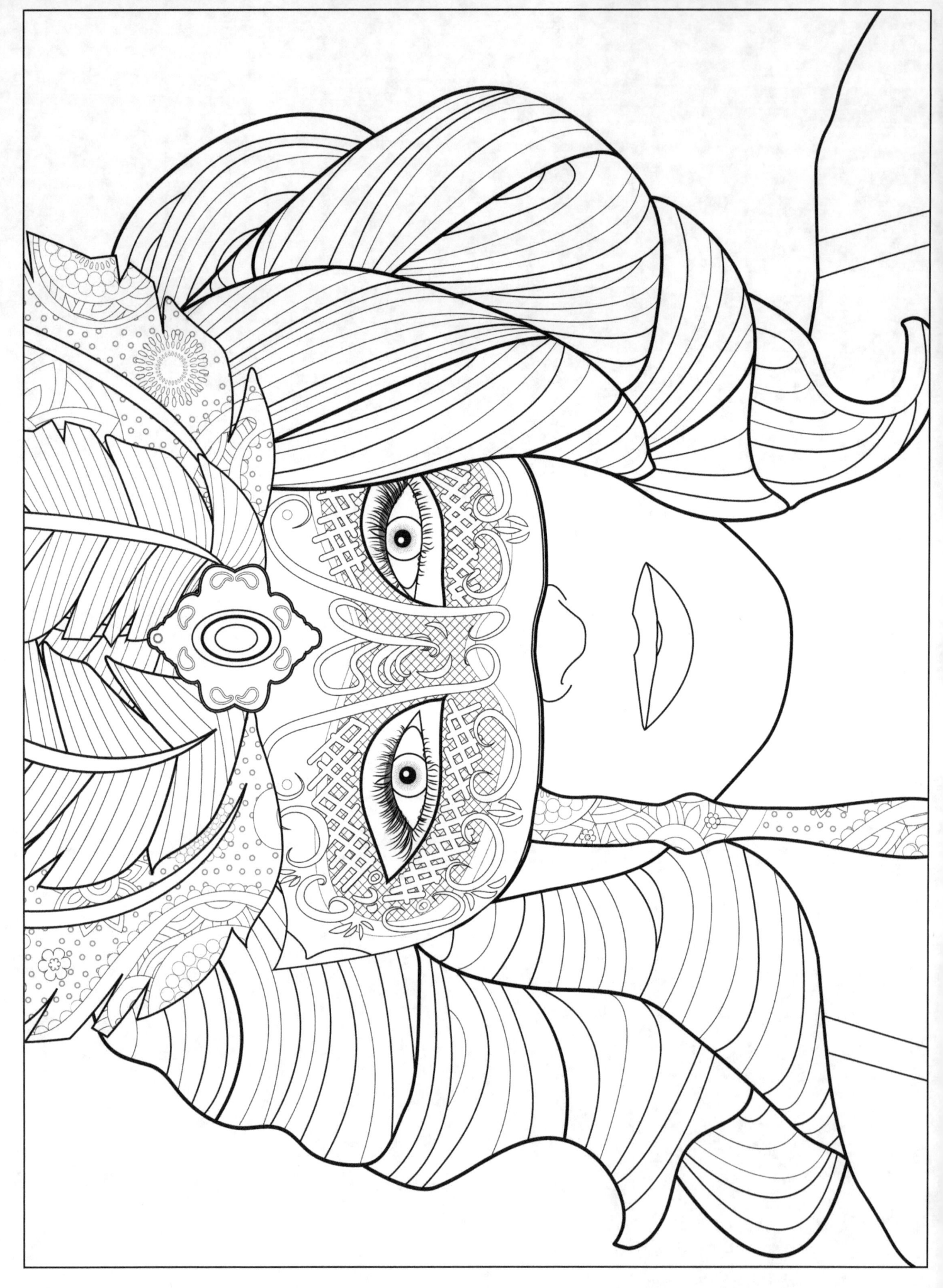

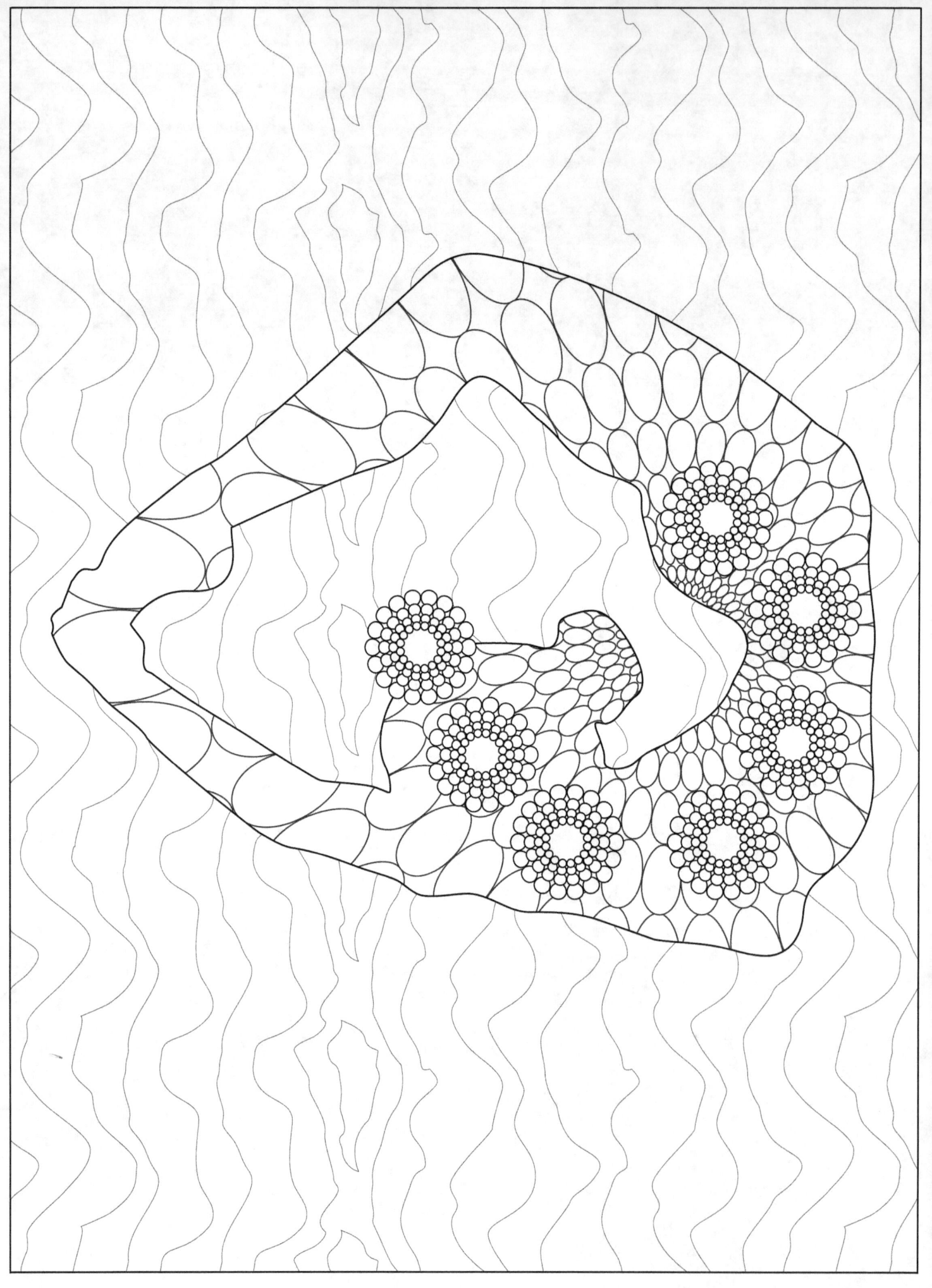

'The Flower of Life' contains the very patterns of creation. From the void, into being; from a crystalized thought, to manifest form.

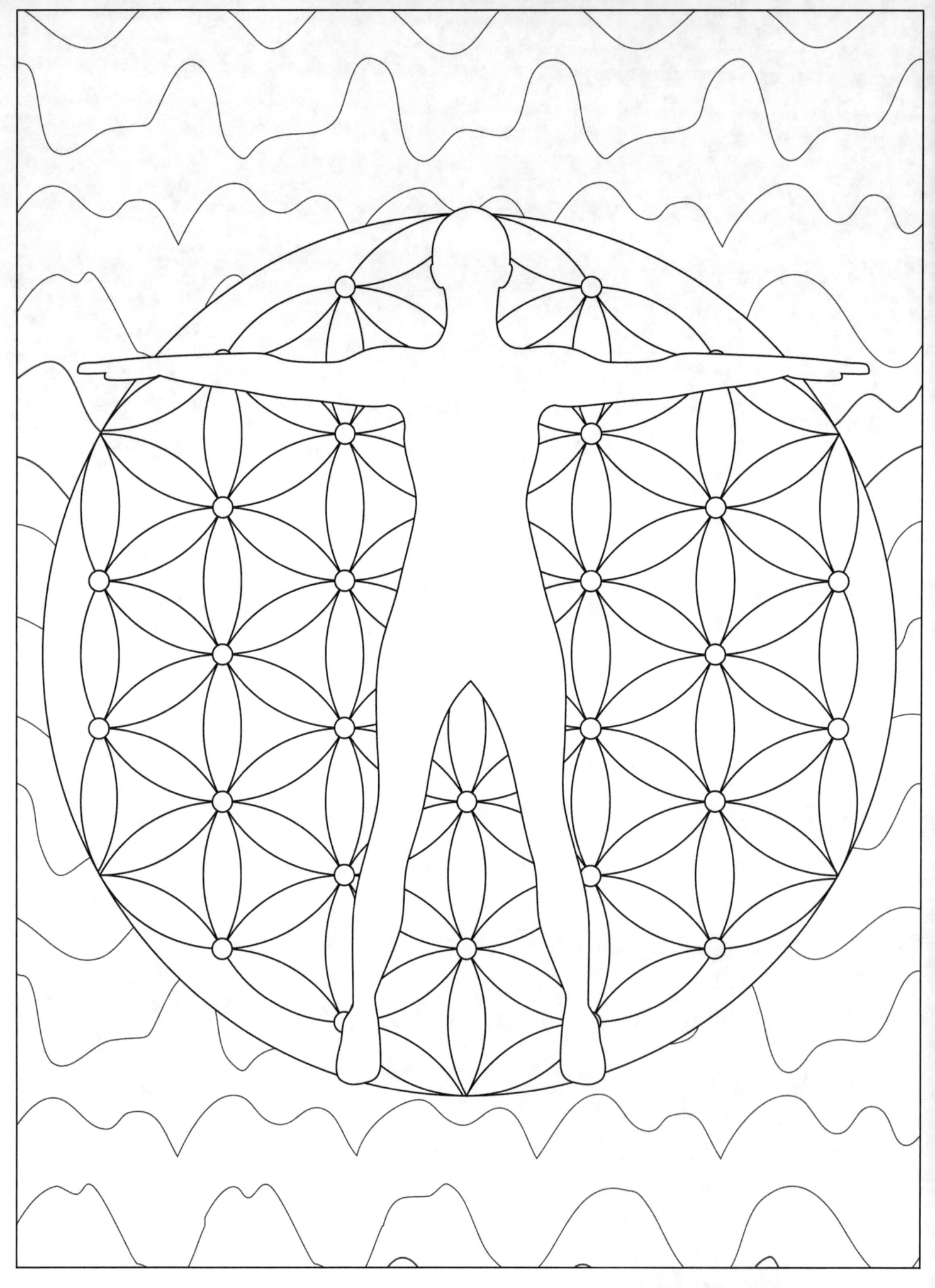

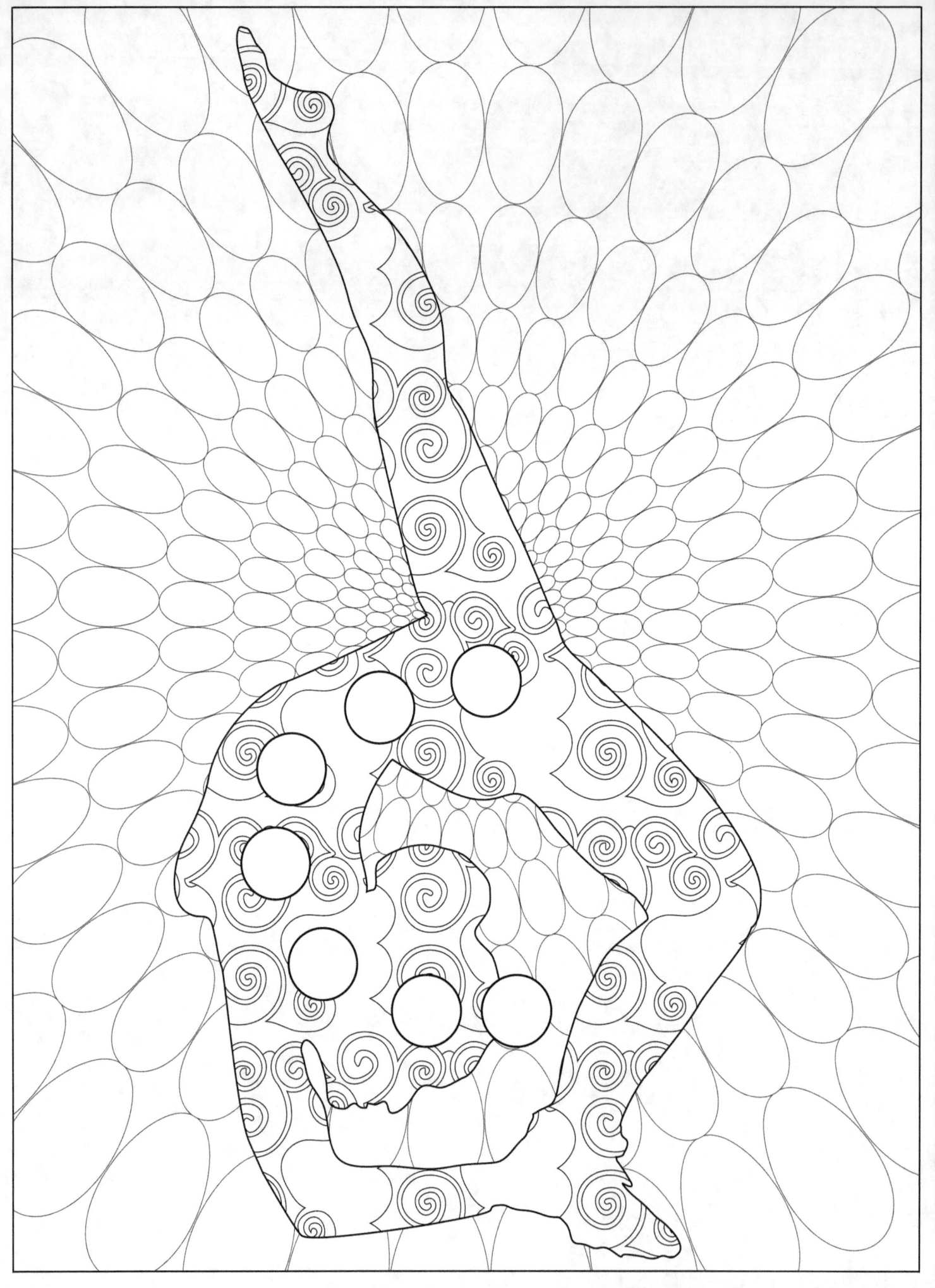

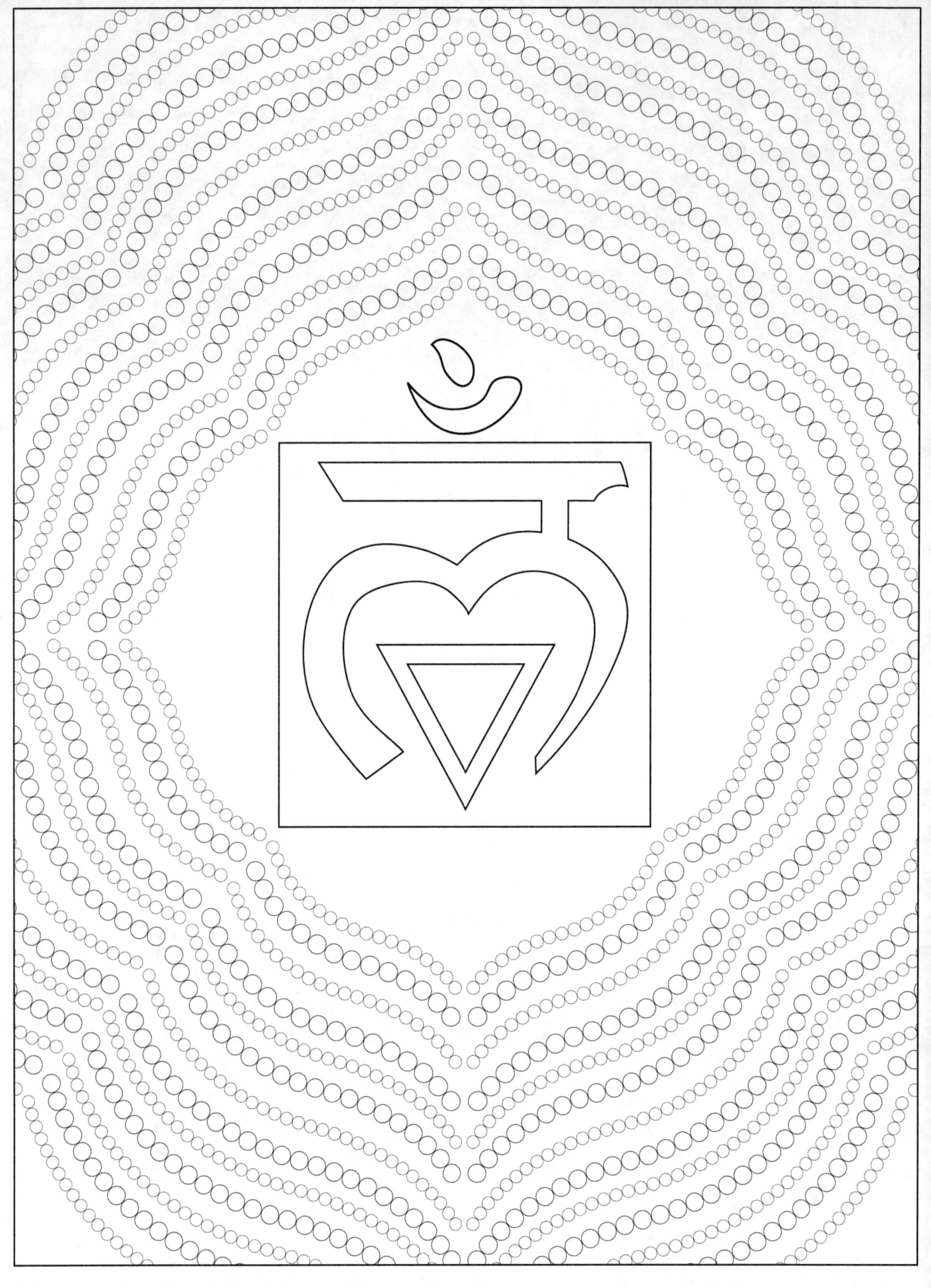

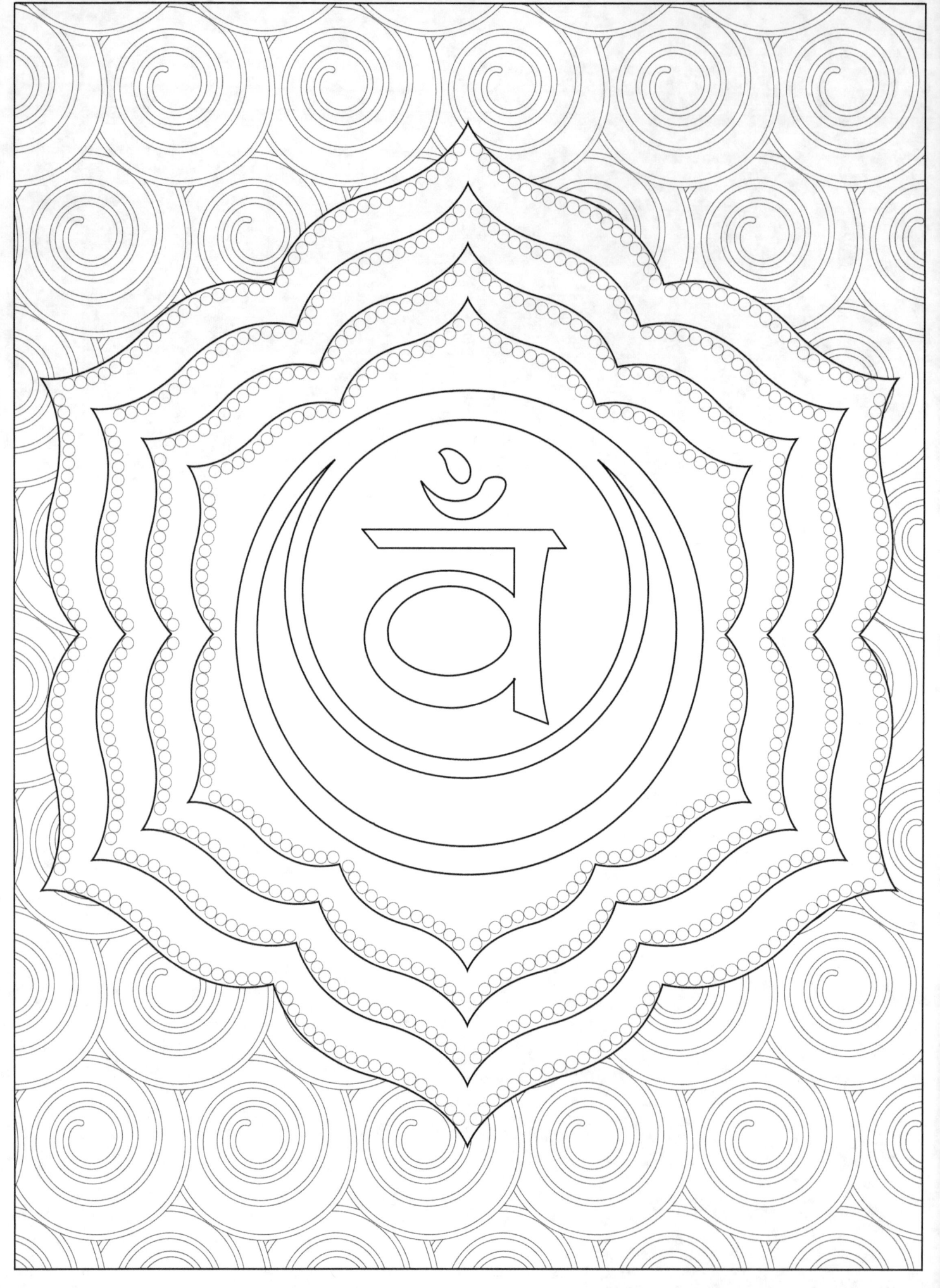

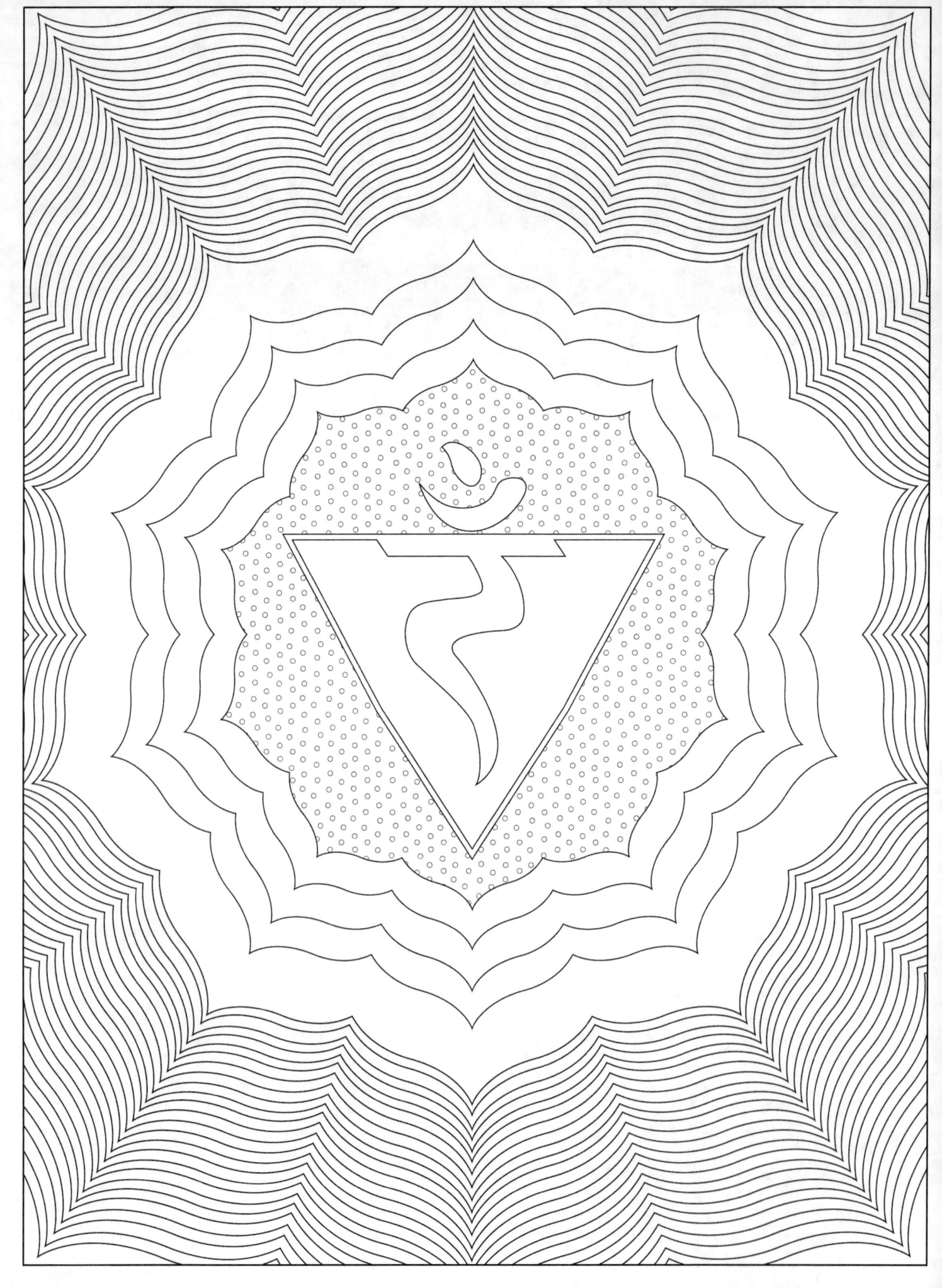

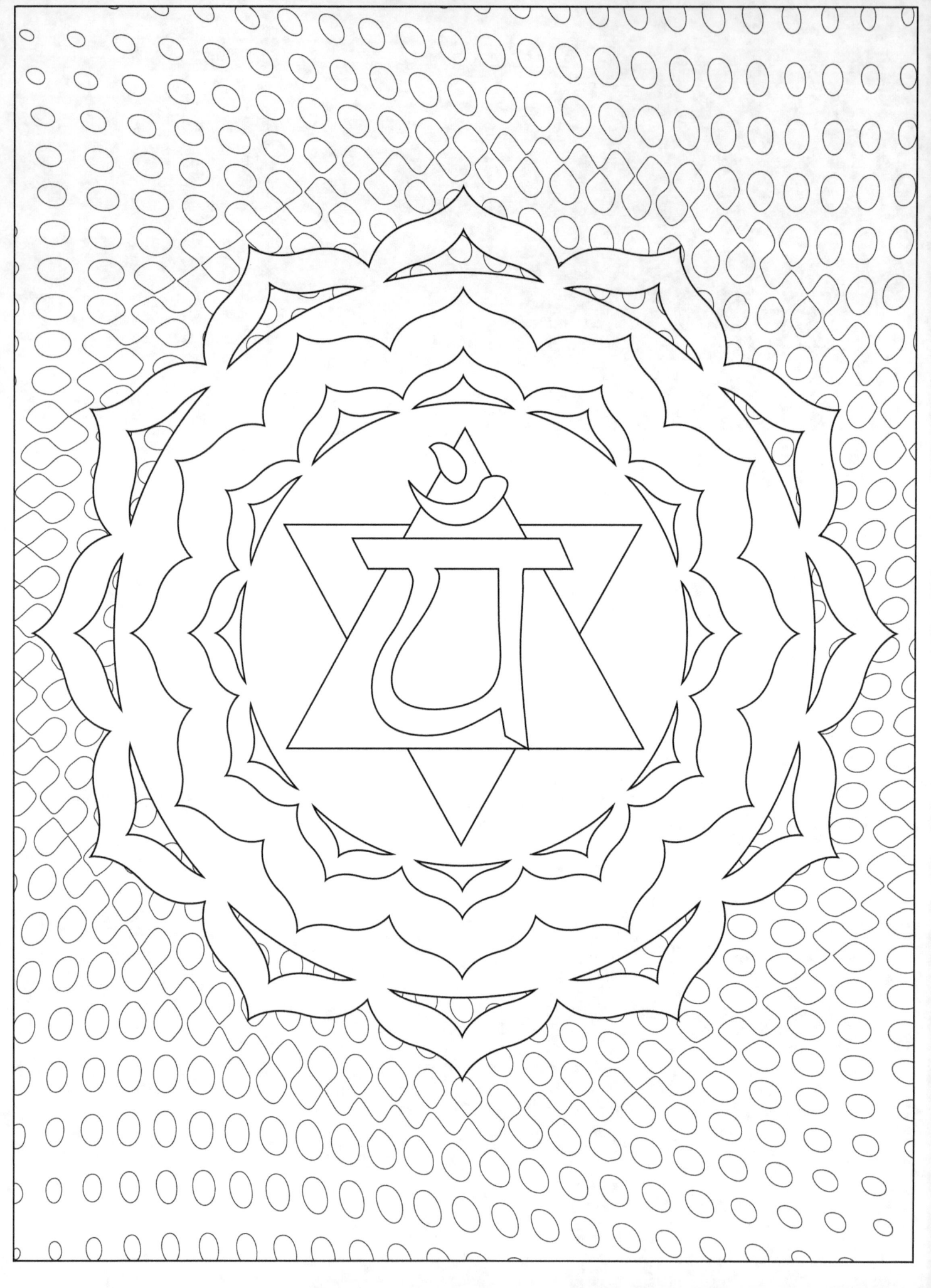

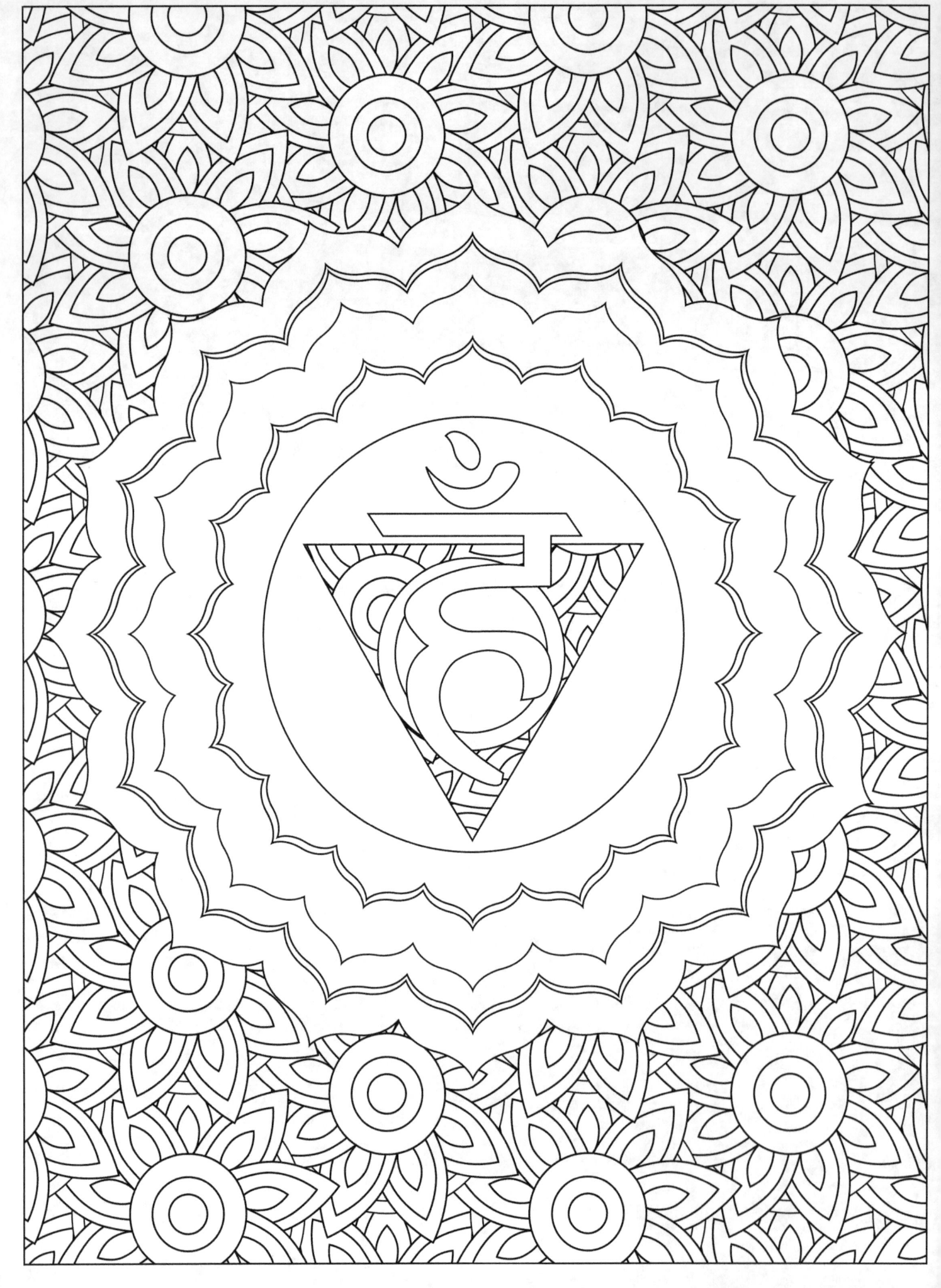

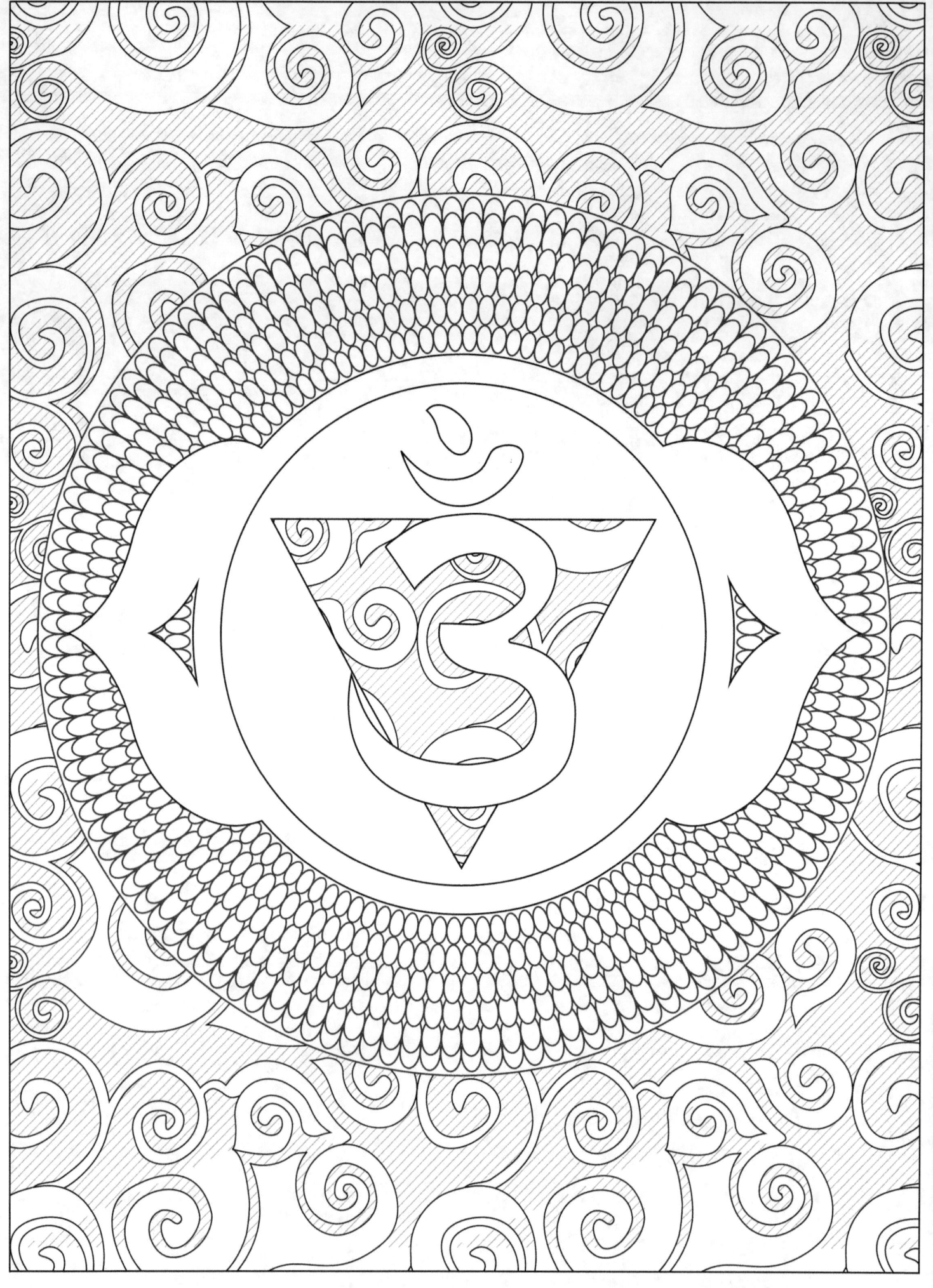

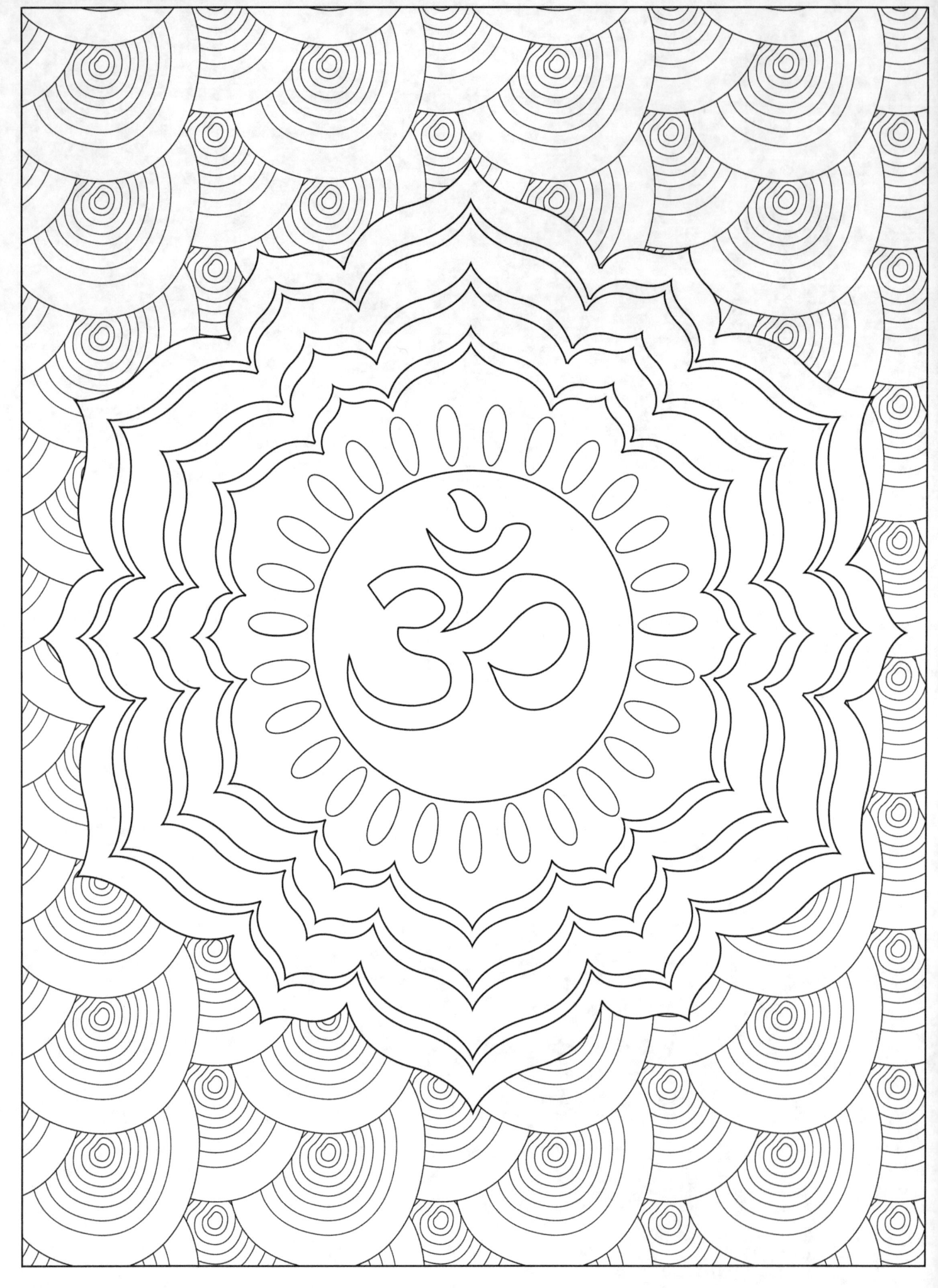

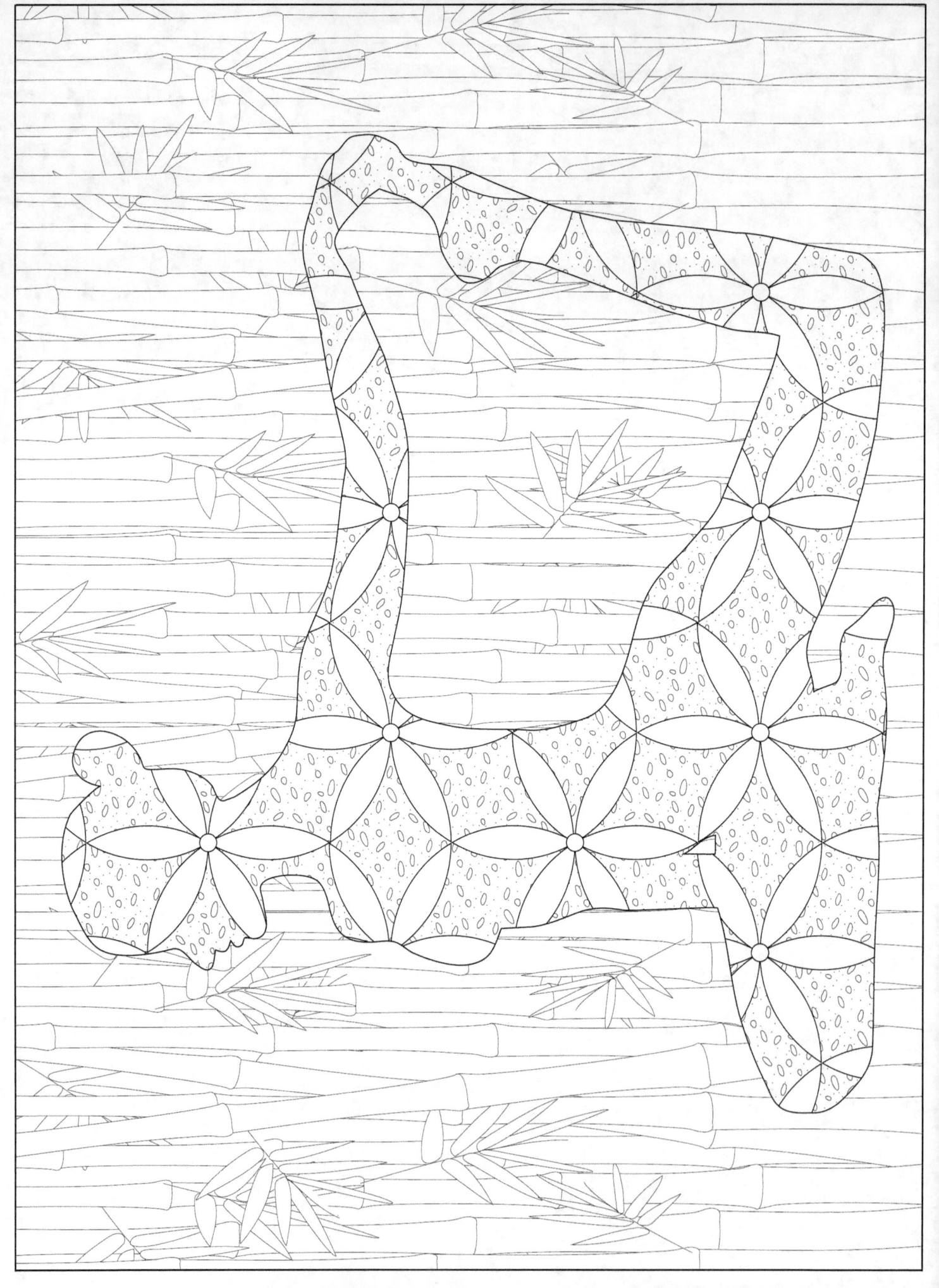

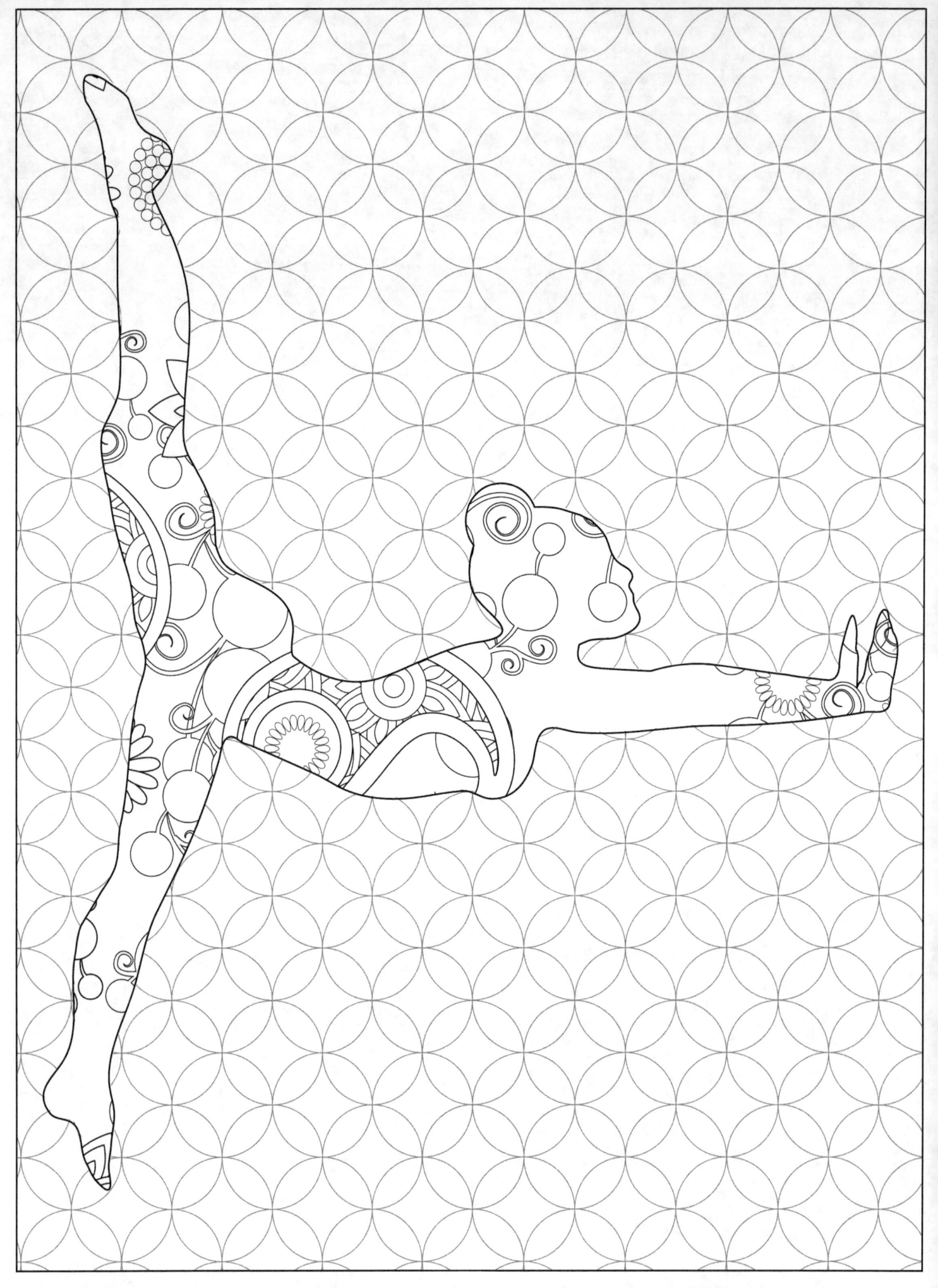

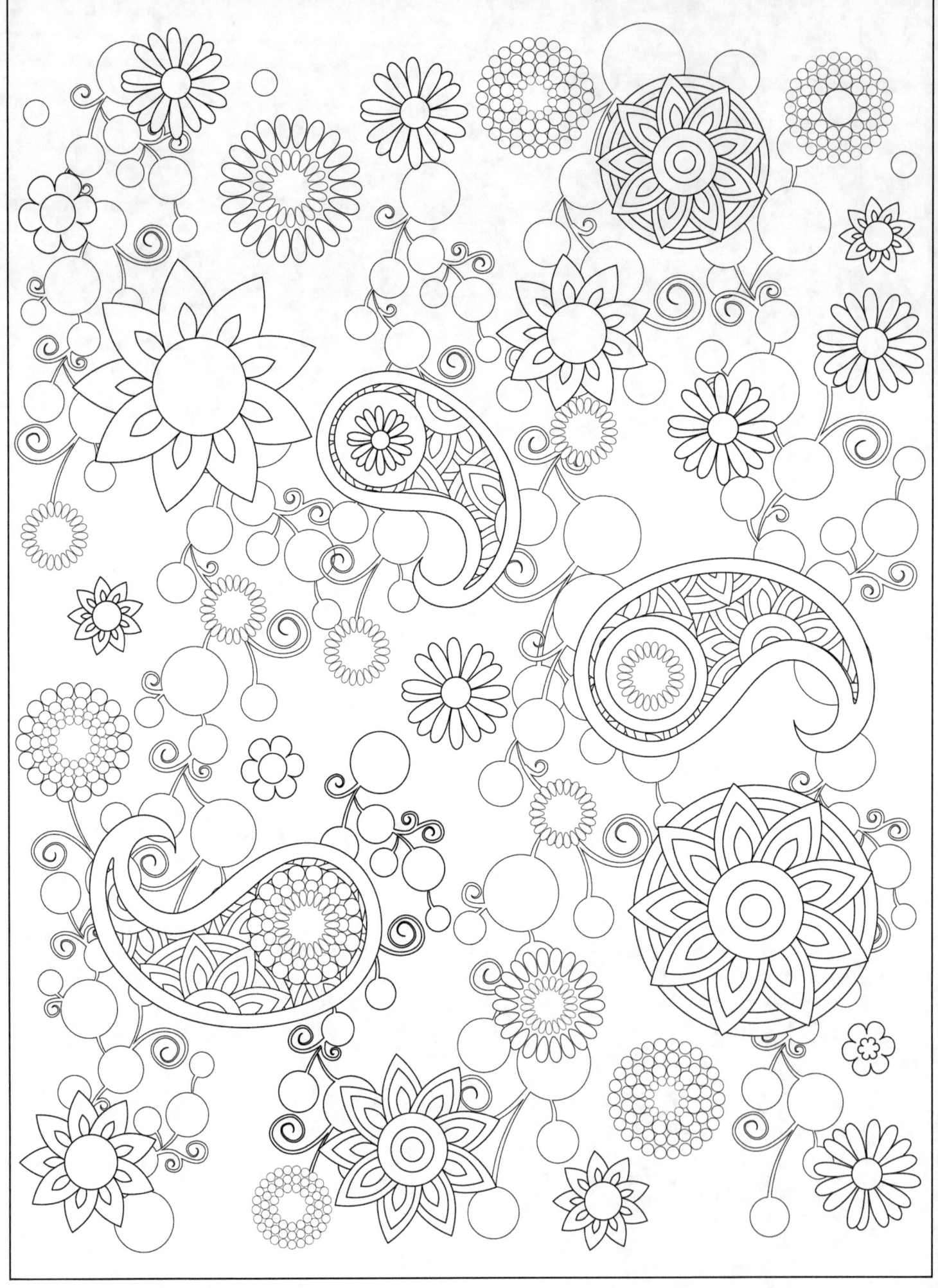

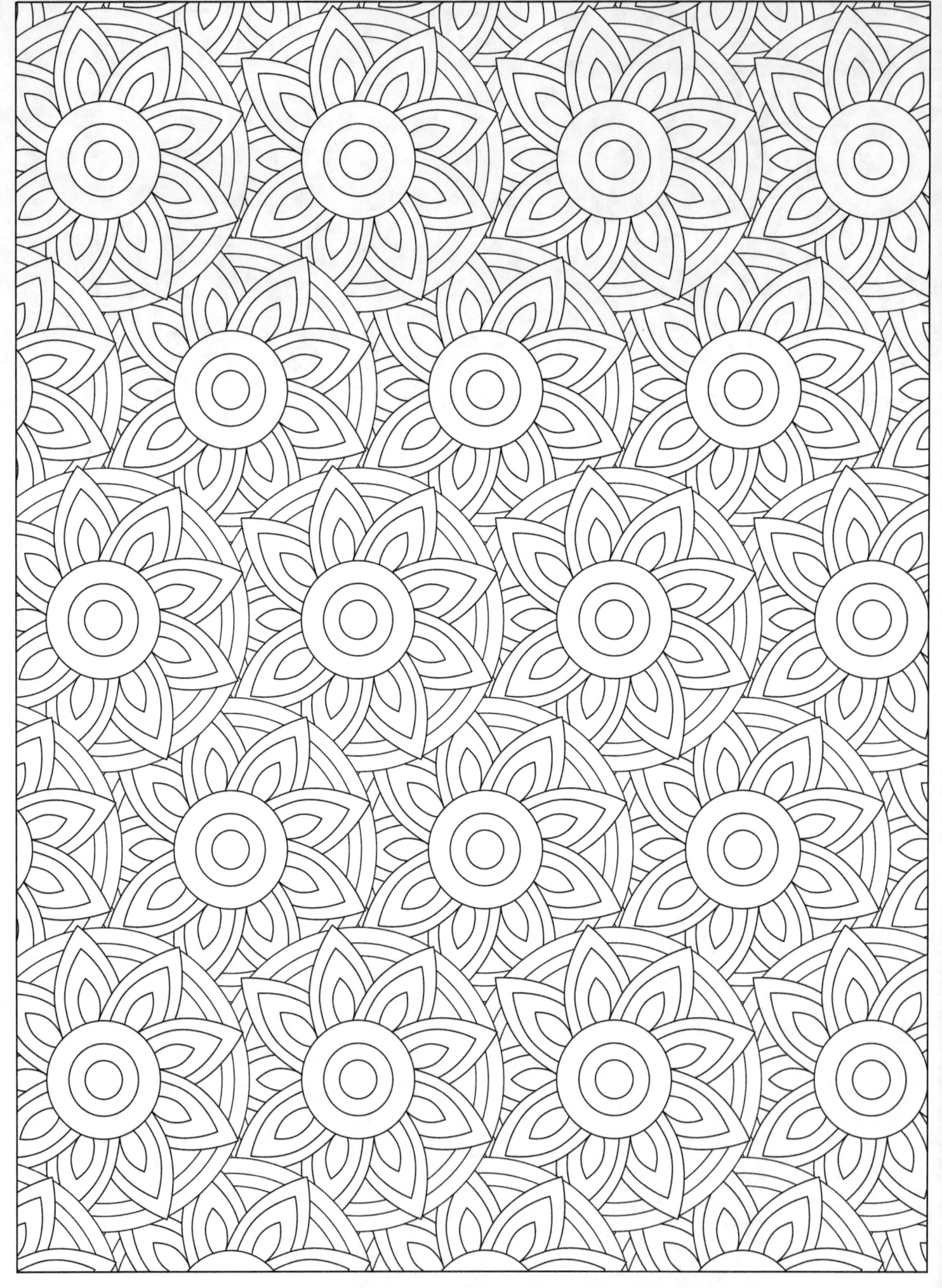

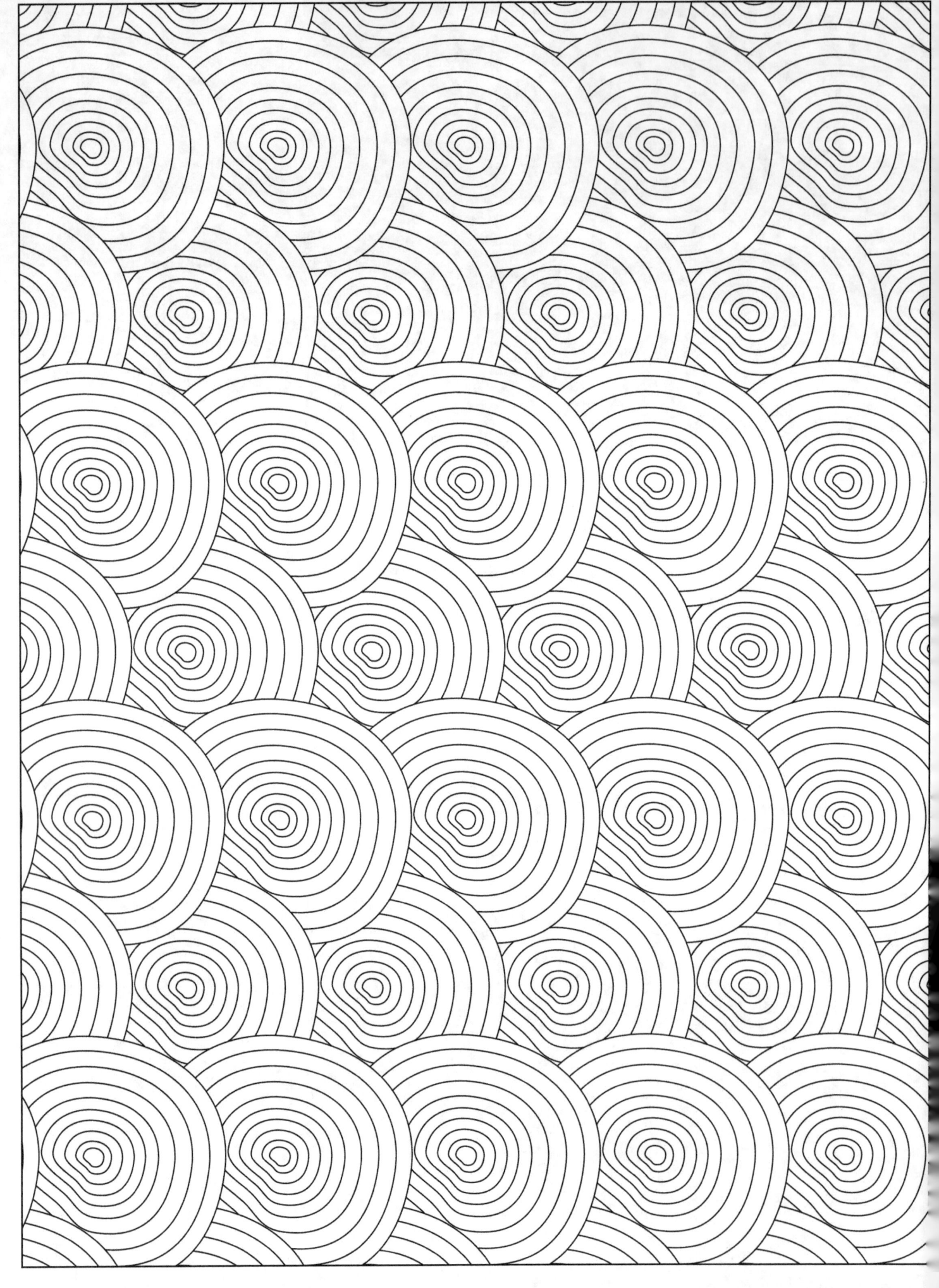

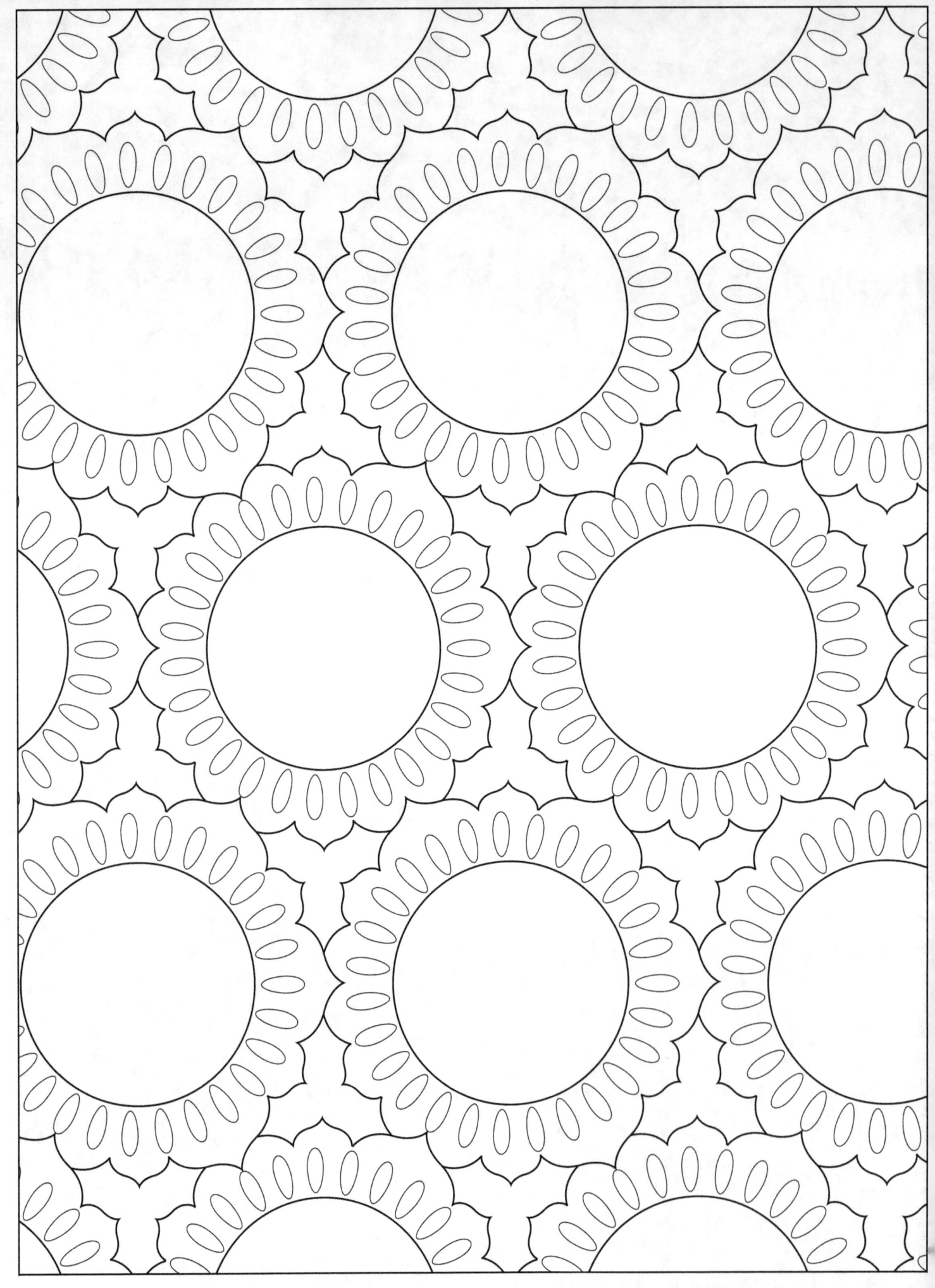